Daily

Between Grades
4 and 5

SUMMER

Activities

Writing: Jill Norris
Content Editing: Marilyn Evans
Allen Associates
Copy Editing: Jessica Cohn
Art Direction: Yuki Meyer
Cover Design: Yuki Meyer
Design/Production: Yuki Meyer
Paula Acojido

EMC 1075

Evan-Moor®
Helping Children Learn

Visit
teaching-standards.com
to view a correlation
of this book.
This is a free service.

**Correlated to
Current Standards**

CPSIA: Asia Pacific Offset Ltd, Kowloon, Hong Kong [1/2021]

Contents

Skills

Skills	Week 1	2	3	4	5	6	7	8	9	10
Reading Comprehension										
Nonfiction	●	●		●	●	●	●		●	●
Fiction	●		●	●	●			●	●	
Make Connections	●	●	●	●	●	●	●	●	●	●
Sequencing Events					●					
Main Idea and Details	●		●			●	●	●	●	
Character and Setting			●			●	●			●
Compare/Contrast	●	●	●			●	●		●	●
Inference	●	●	●	●			●	●	●	●
Context Clues	●	●	●	●			●	●	●	●
Grammar/Usage/Mechanics										
Phonics	●		●	●			●	●		
Spelling	●	●	●	●	●	●	●	●	●	●
Alphabetical Order	●									
Contractions	●		●			●				
Possessives				●	●			●		
Singular/Plural			●	●	●					
Parts of Speech	●	●	●	●	●	●		●	●	●
Conjunctions			●							
Subject/Verb Agreement	●	●	●	●			●	●	●	●
Abbreviations	●						●			
Capitalization	●	●	●	●	●	●	●	●	●	●
Punctuation	●	●	●	●	●	●	●	●	●	●
Verb Tenses	●	●		●						
Compound Sentences	●	●								
Idioms		●								
Quotation Marks		●		●	●	●	●		●	
Syllabification						●				
Vocabulary Development										
Rhyming Words		●								
Silent Letters				●			●			
Compound Words			●			●				
Comparatives/Superlatives						●				
Homophones/Homographs		●				●		●		
Writing										
Write a Sentence	●	●	●	●	●	●	●	●	●	●
Write a Paragraph	●	●	●					●	●	●
Write a List				●	●			●		
Journal Writing	●	●	●	●	●	●	●	●	●	●
Write Questions										●

Daily Summer Activities • EMC 1075 • © Evan-Moor Corp.

Skills	Week 1	2	3	4	5	6	7	8	9	10
Handwriting										
Cursive Writing Practice	●	●	●	●	●	●	●	●	●	●
Math										
Comparing Values				●					●	
Patterning			●		●					
Number Words				●						
Word Problems	●	●	●	●	●	●	●	●	●	●
Place Value	●					●				
Addition	●	●	●		●	●				
Subtraction	●	●			●	●		●		
Multiplication		●	●		●			●		
Division				●	●		●			
Graphs/Grids/Charts		●	●			●	●	●		
Fractions/Decimals			●	●	●	●	●	●	●	
Measurement		●							●	
Shapes/Angles/Symmetry	●			●				●		●
Perimeter/Area			●							
Factors/Multiples							●			
Ratios/Rates	●									●
Geography										
Map-Reading Skills	●		●	●	●		●	●	●	●
Political Maps				●	●		●			●
Physical Maps								●		
Road Maps									●	
Globes	●	●								
Legends		●		●					●	
Compass Rose/Directions		●							●	●
Scales				●						
Latitude and Longitude					●					
Grids					●					
Population						●				
Thinking Skills										
Riddles/Problem Solving	●	●	●	●	●	●	●	●	●	●

About This Book

What's in It

Ten Weekly Sections

Each section contains half-page and full-page activities that help children learn reading, writing, math, geography, spelling, grammar, and critical thinking skills.

Each week, your child will work on the following:

Reading	▶ comprehension activities that include fiction and nonfiction topics
Spell It	▶ an activity to practice the week's spelling words
Write It Right	▶ an editing activity to correct errors in spelling, grammar, and punctuation
Handwriting	▶ a writing activity to practice penmanship skills
Language Bytes	▶ activities that practice language skills, including compound words, parts of speech, subject-verb agreement, and quotation marks
Math Time	▶ activities that practice math skills, including computation, basic geometry, and pre-algebra
In My Own Words	▶ creative writing exercises
Geography	▶ a map activity that tests basic geography concepts
Problem Solving	▶ a critical thinking activity
What Happened Today?	▶ a place to record a memorable moment from the week, and a reading log to record the number of minutes spent reading each day

How to Use It

The short practice lessons in *Daily Summer Activities* prepare your child for the coming school year by making sure that he or she remembers all of the skills and concepts learned in fourth grade. After completing the activities in this book, your child will feel more confident as he or she begins the new school year. You can help your child by following the suggestions below.

Provide Time and Space

Make sure that your child has a quiet place for completing the activities. The practice session should be short and positive. Consider your child's personality and other activities as you decide how and where to schedule daily practice periods.

Encourage and Support

Your response is important to your child's feelings of success. Keep your remarks positive and recognize the effort your child has made. Work through challenging activities and correct mistakes together.

Check in Each Week

Use the weekly record sheet to talk about the most memorable moments and learning experiences of the week and to discuss the books your child is reading.

Be a Model Reader

The most important thing you can do is to make sure your child sees you reading. Read books, magazines, and newspapers. Visit libraries and bookstores. Point out interesting signs, maps, and advertisements wherever you go. Even though your child is an independent reader, you can still share the reading experience by discussing what you read every day.

Go on Learning Excursions

Learning takes place everywhere and through many experiences. Build learning power over the summer by:

- visiting a zoo, local museum, or historic site. Use a guidebook or search online to find points of interest in your area.

- collecting art materials and working together to create a collage, mobile, or scrapbook.

- planning a calendar of summer events. Check off each event as you complete it.

- planting a garden. If you are short on space, plant in containers.

- creating a movie of your child's favorite story. Write a simple script and make basic costumes and props, and recruit friends and family members to be actors. Practice until everyone is comfortable before shooting the video.

Spell It

This list contains all of the weekly spelling words practiced in the book.

A
afternoon
agree
alphabet
although
among
anybody
applesauce
autumn

B
believe
bought
breakfast
brought
busiest

C
ceiling
cent
cheerful
chews
chief
classroom
clue
cough
couldn't
could've
country
cousin

D
danger
daughter
daydream
deceive
describe
destroy
disappoint
doctor
downstairs
dragonfly
due

E
earthquake
enough
everywhere

F
favorite
fearful
flashlight
fright
future

G
giraffe
gnat

H
half
happiness
harmful
haven't
headache
height
hour

K
keyboard
kindest
kneel
knock
knot
knowledge

L
largest
learn
lifeguard
loyal

M
might
minute

N
nephew
news
niece
noise

O
o'clock
officer
often
our
outfield

P
peace
photograph
purchase

Q
quarter
quickly

R
refuse

S
scarecrow
scent
scissors
scoreboard
search
secondhand
several
shoelace
shone
shown
skyscraper
smartest
snowflake
southwest
suddenly
sure
sweatshirt

T
they're
thirsty
threw
through
together
triangle
tried
trouble
truth

U
undercover
uniform
unknown
used
useless

V
variety
voice
voyage

W
which
whose
world
worthless
wrapper
write
written

Y
you're

Daily Summer Activities • EMC 1075 • © Evan-Moor Corp.

Week 2

Color a ⭐ for each page you finish.

Parent's Initials

Monday ☆ ☆

Tuesday ☆ ☆

Wednesday ☆ ☆

Thursday ☆ ☆

Friday ☆ ☆

Spelling Words

shone

shown

cent

scent

peace

hour

our

search

fright

write

threw

through

Write about one thing you did each day.

Monday

Tuesday

Wednesday

Thursday

Friday

Keeping Track

Color a book for every 20 minutes you read.

Monday	**Tuesday**	**Wednesday**	**Thursday**	**Friday**

My favorite book this week was _____.

I liked it because _____

_____.

Daily Summer Activities • EMC 1075 • © Evan-Moor Corp.

Geography

Match the word with the phrase that tells what it means.

physical map •   • a book of maps

land use map •   • a map that shows natural landforms and water

legend •   • a symbol telling directions

atlas •   • a map that shows land used by humans for specific purposes

compass rose •   • an explanation of the symbols used on a map

In My Own Words

Imagine your favorite kind of ice cream. You are standing outside the ice-cream store.

It's a hot day, and you have two dollars in your pocket. Describe what happens next.

Thursday

Week 2

Language Bytes

The underlined phrase in each sentence is an **idiom**. It has a special, nonliteral meaning. Write the meaning of each idiom.

1. Johnny was <u>horsing around</u>.

   _____

2. Tommy is always <u>on the ball</u>.

   _____

3. Mr. Jones's <u>bark is worse than his bite</u>.

   _____

Math Time

Find the answers.

$308 \times 7 =$ _____ $769 \times 4 =$ _____ $853 \times 6 =$ _____ $972 \times 9 =$ _____

$657 \times 1 =$ _____ $896 \times 8 =$ _____ $409 \times 8 =$ _____ $892 \times 6 =$ _____

$738 \times 0 =$ _____ $557 \times 9 =$ _____ $985 \times 5 =$ _____ $850 \times 7 =$ _____

Week 3

Color a ⭐ for each page you finish.

		Parent's Initials
Monday	⭐ ⭐	
Tuesday	⭐ ⭐	
Wednesday	⭐ ⭐	
Thursday	⭐ ⭐	
Friday	⭐ ⭐	

Spelling Words

breakfast

earthquake

flashlight

headache

lifeguard

skyscraper

sweatshirt

shoelace

applesauce

afternoon

daydream

everywhere

Write about one thing you did each day.

Monday
_____

Tuesday
_____

Wednesday
_____

Thursday
_____

Friday

Keeping Track

Color a book for every 20 minutes you read.

Monday	**Tuesday**	**Wednesday**	**Thursday**	**Friday**

My favorite book this week was _____.

I liked it because _____

_____

Dear Anna,

When you look outside your window and see the open spaces, it must be very different from when I look outside my window here in the city. You said that it seems like the prairie reaches out and touches the places where the sky comes down. At my house, all I can see from my windows are houses and streets. I can't see the horizon. It seems as if I could climb from roof to roof to reach the stars.

What is it like at night at your house? There are millions of lights here in the city. It is never really quiet here. There are always noises—buzzes and beeps, honking and hollering. Is nighttime quiet at your house?

I have a little brother just like yours, and it bugs me when he asks the same question over and over. I try to answer his questions, but sometimes I ask him a question instead of giving an answer. That can stop the "why cycle." Do you have the same problem? Do you have any better idea for solving it?

Write back soon.

Your pen pal,
Harriet

1. What kind of place does Harriet live in?

_____

2. Where do you think Anna lives?

_____

3. What do the two girls have in common?

_____

_____

4. What is your house like at night? Write your reply as if Harriet had asked you.

_____

_____

Write It Right

Correct the sentences.

1. clarise antonio and margaret have went to tennis camp since they was seven

    _____

    _____

2. morris leaved his job and moved to dallas texas to be a fire fighter

    _____

    _____

3. the scientists didnt gave up when they couldnt figure out the problem

    _____

    _____

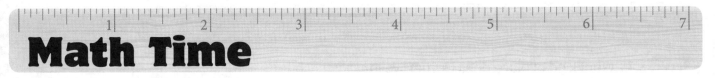

Math Time

Find the area and the perimeter.

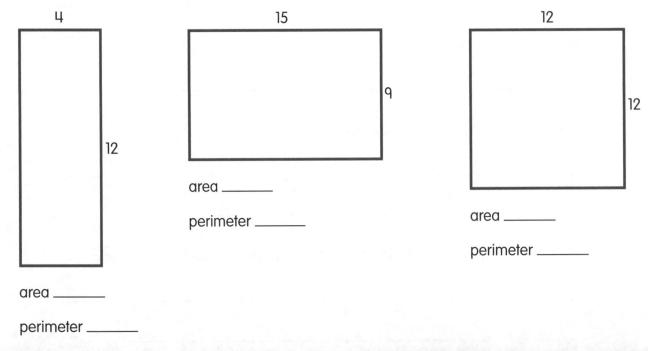

4

12

area _____

perimeter _____

15

9

area _____

perimeter _____

12

12

area _____

perimeter _____

Daily Summer Activities • EMC 1075 • © Evan-Moor Corp.

SPELL IT

Write the two words that make up the compound word. Then explain the meaning of the compound word by writing a sentence that uses the word.

breakfast   break + fast
You break your nightlong fast when you eat breakfast.

1. earthquake   _____ + _____

_____

2. headache   _____ + _____

_____

3. lifeguard   _____ + _____

_____

4. applesauce   _____ + _____

_____

Handwriting

$\mathcal{Y}$ $\mathcal{Y}$ $\mathcal{Y}$ $\mathcal{Y}$ $\mathcal{Y}$ $\mathcal{Y}$

Copy these words.

skyscraper
everywhere

Copy these words.

Yolanda
yesterday

Language Bytes

Use a **conjunction** (**and**, **but**, **or**) to combine each pair of simple sentences into a compound sentence. Use a comma before each conjunction.

1. Aunt Carol baked cookies. The children ate them all.

_____

_____

2. The explorers searched the ice field. They never reached the South Pole.

_____

_____

3. Jana might walk to the park with us. Maybe she will meet us there.

_____

_____

Math Time

Find the answers.

$\dfrac{1}{2} + \dfrac{1}{2} =$ _____

$\dfrac{1}{8} + \dfrac{5}{8} =$ _____

$\dfrac{2}{4} + \dfrac{1}{4} =$ _____

$\dfrac{3}{6} + \dfrac{1}{6} =$ _____

$\dfrac{1}{3} + \dfrac{2}{3} =$ _____

$\dfrac{2}{12} + \dfrac{5}{12} =$ _____

A Letter in the Mail

It was a crisp autumn morning, and I scuffled through the leaves on the sidewalk. I waved to the mailman as he drove off. Then I took a deep breath. Would this be the day? Would the letter finally come?

I turned the key in the lock and slowly swung the door open. On top of the usual fliers announcing the current price of chicken legs and apples and the biggest and best furniture sale were three letters. Would one of the letters have my name on it?

I rubbed the shiny penny in my pocket for good luck. I reached into the box and pulled out the letters. The letter on top was addressed to my mom. It was from the phone company, probably a bill. The next letter was handwritten and addressed to the family. It had to be from Grandma, because nobody else ever wrote handwritten letters.

One more letter… I took a deep breath and looked at the return address. It was from Space Camp. It was addressed to me. This was the letter I had been waiting for! I gulped and felt the smooth, stiff envelope. Was the news inside good or bad? Had I won the scholarship?

I really wanted to go to Space Camp. I had spent hours working on the essay that accompanied the application. Mrs. Johnson had sent a great letter of recommendation. But I knew that lots of other fifth graders were anxiously waiting, too. They all probably really wanted to go to Space Camp. They all had probably spent hours on their essays. Their teachers had probably written great letters of recommendation for them. My stomach fluttered, and my mouth went dry.

What news was inside that envelope?

1. Was the character nervous about opening the letter? Tell how you know.

_____

2. What reasons did the character have for being excited about the Space Camp letter?

_____

_____

3. What reasons did the character have for being worried about the contents of the letter?

_____

_____

Language Bytes

A **common noun** names any person, place, thing, or idea.
A **proper noun** names a specific person, place, thing, or idea.
Proper nouns begin with capital letters.

Write a proper noun to name the following:

your whole name   _____

your school   _____

your town   _____

a song   _____

a movie   _____

a mountain   _____

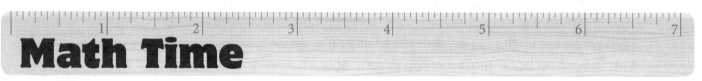

Math Time

Find the answers.

85 × 35 = _____   51 × 93 = _____   84 × 62 = _____   52 × 10 = _____

29 × 15 = _____   124 × 41 = _____   73 × 27 = _____   98 × 40 = _____

73 × 29 = _____   128 × 5 = _____   219 × 8 = _____   106 × 5 = _____

(Work Space)

Geography

Antarctica Cross Section

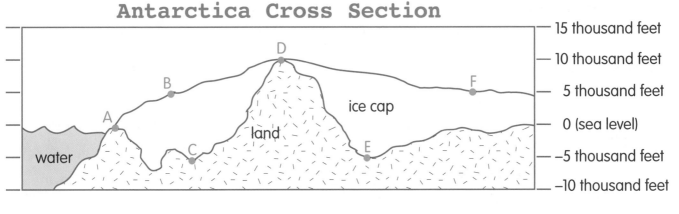

1. What is the approximate elevation of these points?

   Point A _____   Point D _____

   Point B _____   Point E _____

   Point C _____   Point F _____

2. Do you know the elevation of the place where you live? If not, try to find out.

In My Own Words

> You have just received a letter congratulating you on winning a full scholarship to Space Camp. You will learn about spaceflight as you participate in the same kind of training that real astronauts complete. The letter asks you to write a paragraph either accepting or declining the offer. What would you say? Write the paragraph here.

Language Bytes

Singular nouns name one person, place, thing, or idea. **Plural nouns** name more than one. Complete this paragraph using the plural form of the missing words.

Peter looked around the _____. There were _____ and
                              cage   kitten

_____, _____, and _____. There were even some
     puppy   mouse   hamster

_____. The SPCA had _____ for everyone. He walked up and down
     sheep   animal

the _____, trying to make up his mind. The _____ watched him with
      aisle   animal

bright _____. Some voiced _____, and some moved back into the
      eye   greeting

_____ of their _____. Peter wished that he could adopt them all.
   corner   cubicle

Math Time

Complete the input/output charts.

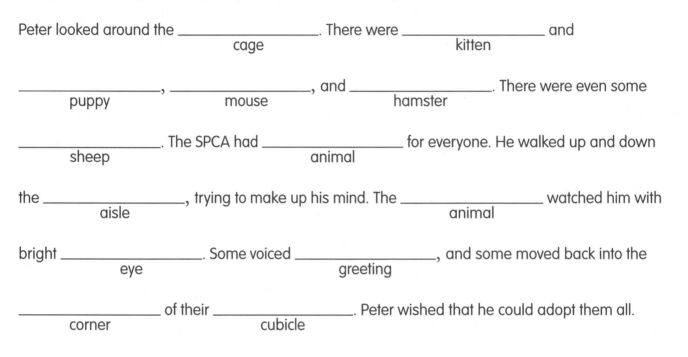

Input	8	10	12	
Output	2	4		8

Input	5	10	15	
Output	1	2	3	

Input	3	6	9			
Output	4	8	12			

Daily Summer Activities • EMC 1075 • © Evan-Moor Corp.

Language Bytes

Find the groups of words that are sentences. Add end punctuation and write the word **sentence** on the line following each complete sentence. Then add words to each fragment to make it a sentence. Write your new sentences on the lines at the bottom.

Climbed the rock and rested   _____

The leaves rustled in the wind   _____

The basketball swished through the net   _____

Pete, Anna, and Paul   _____

Did he go home   _____

_____

_____

_____

Math Time

Find the answers.

1. Andy likes to ride his bike. He can ride from his house to school in 10 minutes, from school to Juan's house in 12 minutes, from Juan's house to the mall in 7 minutes, and from the mall to his house in 17 minutes. How long will it take Andy to ride from school to the mall if he rides by Juan's house on the way?   _____

2. Carla wants to see a movie with her friends to celebrate her birthday. The matinee costs $2.50, and the evening show costs $4.00. If her mother gives her $30.00 to pay for tickets, how many people (including Carla) can go to the matinee? to the evening show?

   _____ matinee

   _____ evening show

3. Marcos is 48 inches tall. His younger brother, Jose, is 9 inches shorter than Marcos. His older brother, Raul, is 16 inches taller than Jose. How tall is Raul?

   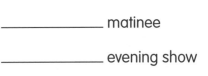

   _____ inches

   _____ feet and inches

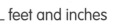

Buried Treasure

Draw a line showing the way to the buried treasure. Each box is one pace.
Draw an **X** where you should dig.

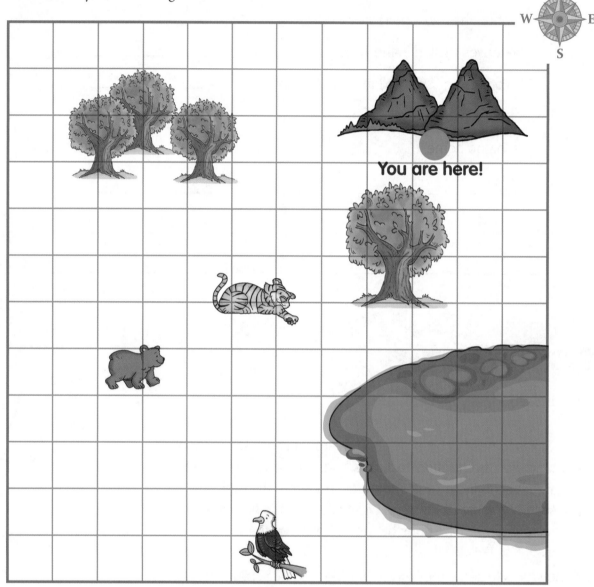

1. Four paces south
2. Six paces west
3. Three paces north
4. Two paces west
5. Eight paces south

6. Five paces east
7. Seven paces north
8. One step east
9. Three paces north
10. Dig!

What do you think you will find?

_____

_____

Daily Summer Activities • EMC 1075 • © Evan-Moor Corp.

Week 4

Color a ⭐ for each page you finish.

Parent's Initials

Monday ☆ ☆

Tuesday ☆ ☆

Wednesday ☆ ☆

Thursday ☆ ☆

Friday ☆ ☆

Spelling Words

knot

kneel

knock

knowledge

unknown

gnat

autumn

brought

daughter

scissors

wrapper

written

Write about one thing you did each day.

Monday

_____

Tuesday

_____

Wednesday

_____

Thursday

_____

Friday

Keeping Track

Color a book for every 20 minutes you read.

Monday	Tuesday	Wednesday	Thursday	Friday

My favorite book this week was _____.

I liked it because _____

_____.

Allen Say

© Christoph Rieger

Allen Say was born in Yokohama, Japan. When he was six years old, he decided that he wanted to be a cartoonist. However, the world was at war. In the midst of the war, he attended seven different elementary schools. When the war ended, Allen was sent to live with his grandmother. He didn't get along with her, so he was allowed to live alone in a one-room apartment. He was twelve years old when he apprenticed himself to a famous Japanese cartoonist, Noro Shinpei. He spent the next four years drawing and painting.

When Allen was sixteen, his father moved with Allen to the United States. Allen went to a military school in California for one year and then struck out on his own. He moved from job to job, city to city, and school to school. He painted his way through California before he opened a photography studio.

Allen Say has had a long and successful career as a writer, an illustrator, and a photographer. Many of his books tell about parts of his life. His autobiographical story, *Grandfather's Journey*, won the Caldecott Medal in 1994. He has said that it is a joyous experience to tell a story with his brush.

....

1. What was Allen Say's ambition?

_____

2. What was unusual about young Allen's life?

_____

3. What does it mean to "apprentice oneself to another person"?

_____

4. What do you do that is a joyous experience?

_____

Check your public library for a book written by Allen Say. *The Apprentice's Ink* is a chapter book that tells about his time as an apprentice.

Write It Right

Correct the sentences.

1. how many pancakes does you want the cook ask us

   _____

   _____

2. prof mansour read a poem called family time and then he singed a song called we is family

   _____

   _____

3. mr williams how much does these flowers cost carmen asked

   _____

   _____

Math Time

Find the answers.

$48 \div 8 =$ _____ $56 \div 7 =$ _____ $46 \div 2 =$ _____ $72 \div 6 =$ _____ $65 \div 5 =$ _____

$64 \div 4 =$ _____ $78 \div 3 =$ _____ $104 \div 8 =$ _____ $90 \div 6 =$ _____ $128 \div 8 =$ _____

$81 \div 3 =$ _____ $105 \div 7 =$ _____ $80 \div 5 =$ _____ $38 \div 2 =$ _____ $76 \div 4 =$ _____

$117 \div 9 =$ _____ $84 \div 7 =$ _____ $210 \div 5 =$ _____ $81 \div 9 =$ _____ $34 \div 2 =$ _____

SPELL IT

Cross out the silent letter or letters in each of the words below. Then use the words to complete the sentences.

> knot   daughter   unknown   kneel   brought   written   scissors

1. Kate had to _____ down to untie the _____ in her shoelace.

2. Mrs. Yang's _____ used a pair of _____ to cut the ribbon

   on the gift she had _____ her.

3. This poem was _____ long ago by an _____ poet.

Handwriting

Copy these phrases in your best handwriting.

Marvelous, magnificent Monday.
Totally terrific Tuesday.
Wild and wonderful Wednesday.
Thoroughly thrilling Thursday.
And finally, fun-filled Friday.
What a week!

Language Bytes

Most **plural nouns** end in **s**, but some nouns have irregular plural forms or do not change at all. Use the correct plural form for each singular noun in the sentences below.

1. All the _____ and _____ got into the lifeboats before
   woman   child

   the _____.
   man

2. Be sure to wash your _____ and brush your _____
   foot   tooth

   before you go to bed.

3. The people saw flocks of _____. There were _____ and herds
   goose   moose

   of _____ in the forest, too.
   deer

Math Time

Write the following numbers in standard form.

two hundred eighty-nine   _____

one thousand five hundred thirty-five   _____

seven hundred seventy-two   _____

ten thousand sixty-nine   _____

Write the following numbers in word form.

682 _____

897 _____

1,268 _____

12,043 _____

Daily Summer Activities • EMC 1075 • © Evan-Moor Corp.

Cut and Paste a Story

When Lois Ehlert went to art school, she discovered that she liked cutting and pasting better than she liked drawing. It was hard to move the parts of a drawing around, but if shapes were cut out of paper they could be moved before they were glued down. So Ms. Ehlert focused on creating collages. She glued scraps of fabric, ribbon, wire, wrapping paper, plastic, cardboard, seeds, buttons, tree bark, and cardboard flaps. She formed the "found" materials into pictures of the animals, flowers, and trees she loved.

Lois Ehlert's colorful collages illustrate the children's books she has written. When she wrote *Eating the Alphabet*, she spent a year visiting her local grocery store, buying fruits and vegetables, creating bright, bold collages, and eating! Ms. Ehlert has said that every book requires hard work, endless research, and a special idea for presenting the information to her readers.

1. Why did Lois Ehlert like cutting and pasting better than drawing?

   _____

   _____

2. What is a collage?

   _____

   _____

3. What does "found" materials mean in this article?

   _____

   _____

4. Lois Ehlert has said that everyone needs a special space for keeping all the things for creating. What things would you keep in your special space? What would you create with those things?

   _____

   _____

Language Bytes

The **tense** of a verb tells when an action occurs.

Underline the verbs in the paragraph below.
Write **P** over the verb if it happened in the **past**.
Write **PR** over the verb if it happens in the **present**.
Write **F** over the verb if it will happen in the **future**.

My cousin promised that she will come for the weekend. She called me last

night and said she is coming this evening. She will arrive about 7:00 p.m. Mom is fixing

her favorite dessert as a surprise. We will have a party while she is here.

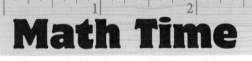

Math Time

Draw the lines of symmetry for each shape.
Then write how many the shape has.

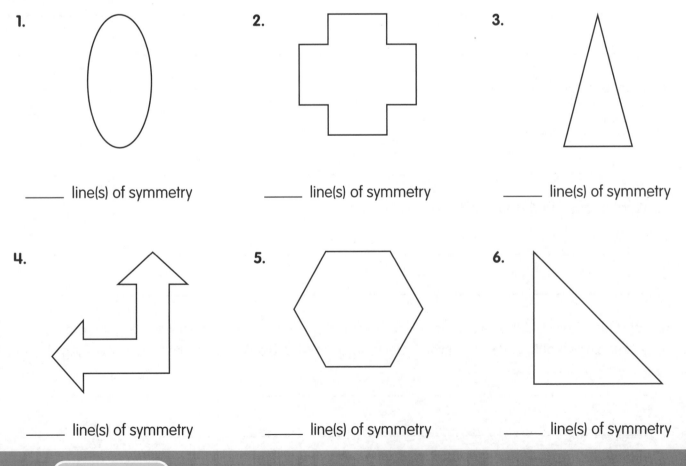

1.

_____ line(s) of symmetry

2.

_____ line(s) of symmetry

3.

_____ line(s) of symmetry

4.

_____ line(s) of symmetry

5.

_____ line(s) of symmetry

6.

_____ line(s) of symmetry

Geography

Use a ruler and the map scale to measure the distance between these locations.

Brazil

From	To	Approximate Distance
Rio de Janeiro	Brasília	_____
São Paulo	Pôrto Alegre	_____
Pôrto Velho	Brasília	_____

Find two cities on the map that are about 400 km apart.

_____

_____

Brazil

• Manaus
• Belém
Fortaleza •
• Pôrto Velho
Recife •

Brazil

☼ Brasília
• Goiânia
Belo Horizonte •
Rio de Janeiro •
São Paulo •

KEY

⭐ Capital
● City

0   400 km

Pôrto Alegre •

In My Own Words

Make a new word. Use parts of existing words if you'd like.

_____

What does your word mean? Write its definition.

_____

Use your word in a sentence.

_____

Write about what might happen if you used your new word in a conversation.

_____

Language Bytes

We add **ed** to many verbs to make the past tense. Other verbs have spelling changes. These are called **irregular verbs**.

Write the past tense of these verbs.

present	past		present	past
begin	_____		choose	_____
grow	_____		eat	_____
run	_____		know	_____
throw	_____		drink	_____
think	_____		write	_____
make	_____		swing	_____

Math Time

Can you put the numbers in order?

1. Rewrite these numbers in order from smallest to largest.

8.00	8.30	0.800	0.83
_____	_____	_____	_____
smallest			largest

57,327	5,703,275	573,275	5,732
_____	_____	_____	_____
smallest			largest

2. Write **>**, **<**, or **=** in the circles to make a true statement.

65.73 ◯ 65.81   2 ◯ 1.3   81.0 ◯ 81.00   3 × 4 ◯ 6 × 2

Week 5

Color a ⭐ for each page you finish.

			Parent's Initials
Monday	☆	☆	
Tuesday	☆	☆	
Wednesday	☆	☆	
Thursday	☆	☆	
Friday	☆	☆	

Spelling Words

believe

chief

niece

deceive

ceiling

agree

might

height

tried

describe

triangle

variety

Write about one thing you did each day.

Monday
_____

Tuesday
_____

Wednesday
_____

Thursday
_____

Friday

Keeping Track

Color a book for every 20 minutes you read.

Monday	Tuesday	Wednesday	Thursday	Friday

My favorite book this week was _____.

I liked it because _____

_____.

The Science Project

Just before the bell rang, Mr. Nielsen said, "Don't forget that your science projects are due a week from today."

Jose thought about his project. A few days ago, he had found frog eggs at the pond near his house. He had scooped up a dozen or so eggs and some pond water in an empty jar. At home, he placed the jar on top of the refrigerator to stay warm. The eggs looked like small black beads in white jelly.

Each day, Jose looked at the eggs through a magnifying glass and drew what he saw. Day by day, he watched the jelly part of the eggs get smaller as the tadpoles grew in the black centers. Soon he could see heads and tails, and the tadpoles began to move. His science book said that the jelly part was food for the growing tadpoles.

The next Thursday, the first of the eggs hatched. A tiny tadpole stuck itself to a leaf of the pond plant Jose had put in the jar. It had no mouth yet, but Jose could see fingerlike gills behind its head.

By Friday, four more eggs had hatched. Jose carefully carried the jar to school, along with his day-by-day drawings and his journal of the changes he'd seen.

"This is a fine project, Jose," said Mr. Nielsen. "You must have given it a lot of thought."

Number these sentences in the order in which they happened.

_____ The tadpoles began to hatch.

_____ On Friday, Jose took his science project to school.

_____ Mr. Nielsen liked Jose's science project.

_____ Jose found frog eggs in the pond and took some home in a jar.

_____ The young tadpoles had gills but no mouths.

_____ Each day the black part of the eggs grew to look more like tadpoles.

Language Bytes

Some **possessives** do not need apostrophes.
Circle the possessive form in each of these sentences.

1. The dog wagged its tail.

2. We spent our summer at camp.

3. My hat is on the table.

4. The roosters held their heads high.

Write a sentence that uses a possessive that does <u>not</u> need an apostrophe.

_____

_____

Math Time

Find the answers.

Work Space

1. Rafael can run one mile in 8.5 minutes. If he keeps up this pace, how long will it take him to run 5 miles?

   _____

2. Maria is selling T-shirts for her choir. Each shirt sells for $8. The choir keeps half of that as profit. If she sells 14 shirts, how much money will she have earned for the choir?

   _____

3. Abby is half as old as her dad, but twice as old as her brother Sal. If Sal is 11, how old is their dad?

   _____

⸺Geography⸺

Find the towns or cities located at these points.

1. 35°S, 138°E

_____

2. 36°S, 149°E

_____

3. 43°S, 147°E

_____

4. 38°S, 145°E

_____

Australia

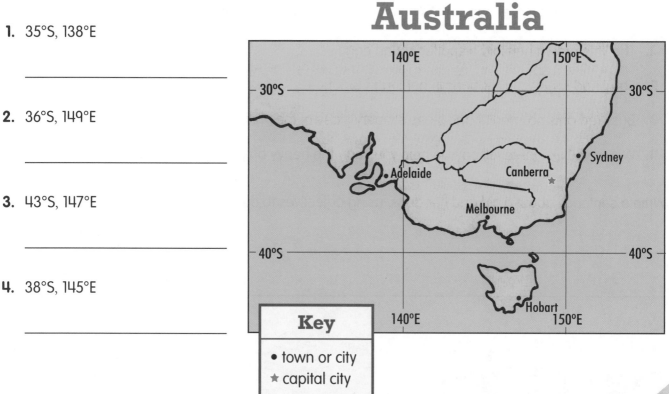

Key

- • town or city
- ★ capital city

In My Own Words

How Do You Play?

Write the directions for your favorite summer game.

- • Start from the beginning.
- • Make the directions easy to understand.
- • Include a list of any special equipment needed.

Language Bytes

A **comma** is used to separate two or more adjectives listed together, unless one of them refers to size, color, or number. Add commas to the sentences below.

1. The little brown hen laid a spotted round egg.

2. Sami had bright curly ribbons in her long black hair.

3. Busy red ants scurried up the steep slippery sides of their hill.

4. Would you like three tall boys to help you carry the heavy bulging grocery bags?

Write a sentence about a girl and her dogs, using adjectives to describe how many and what kind.

_____

_____

Math Time

Draw a model for each problem. Then write the answer.

$\frac{1}{2} + \frac{1}{2} =$	$\frac{1}{4} + \frac{3}{4} =$	$\frac{1}{3} + \frac{2}{3} =$
$\frac{3}{4} + \frac{3}{4} =$	$\frac{1}{6} + \frac{5}{6} =$	$\frac{1}{8} + \frac{3}{8} =$

Daily Summer Activities • EMC 1075 • © Evan-Moor Corp.

Language Bytes

Use **this** with singular nouns. Use **these** with plural nouns.
Complete each sentence using **this** or **these**.

1. _____ slice of cake is yummy.

2. Will you help me put _____ chairs away?

3. _____ is the steepest hill in the neighborhood.

4. I want to put _____ books in my backpack.

Write a sentence using **this** as an adjective.

_____

Write a sentence using **these** as an adjective.

_____

Math Time

Draw a model for each problem. Then write the answer.

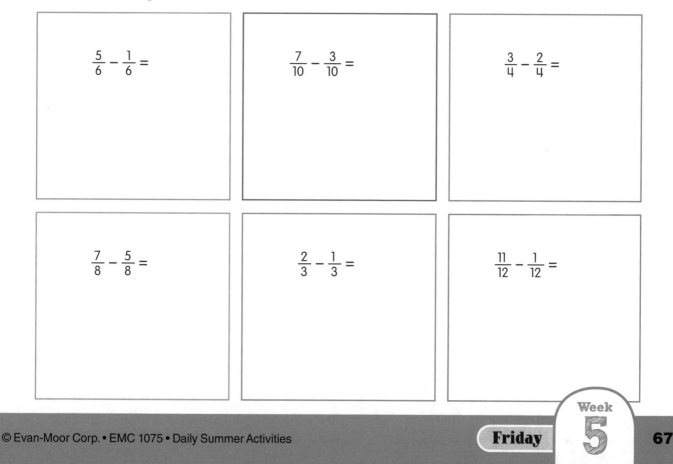

$$\frac{5}{6} - \frac{1}{6} =$$

$$\frac{7}{10} - \frac{3}{10} =$$

$$\frac{3}{4} - \frac{2}{4} =$$

$$\frac{7}{8} - \frac{5}{8} =$$

$$\frac{2}{3} - \frac{1}{3} =$$

$$\frac{11}{12} - \frac{1}{12} =$$

Syllogisms

Long ago in Greece, a famous thinker named Aristotle invented the **syllogism**. A syllogism has three parts. Facts are given in the first two parts. The third part is a new idea taken from the facts in the first two parts.

    Example: All birds have feathers.
                         Chickens are birds.
                         Therefore, chickens have feathers.

A syllogism can be valid without being true.

    Example: All babies are cute.
                         No cute things cry.
                         Therefore, no babies cry.

Write the third line for each of the following syllogisms.
Mark whether you think the syllogism is true or false.

All children like bubble gum.
All girls are children.

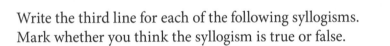

Therefore, _____.   True   False

All kinds of fruit are sweet.
Lemons are a kind of fruit.

Therefore, _____.   True   False

All stars are in the sky.
The sun is a star.

Therefore, _____.   True   False

All apples grow on trees.
Granny Smiths are apples.

Therefore, _____.   True   False

Week 6

Color a ⭐ for each page you finish.

Parent's Initials

Monday	⭐ ⭐	
Tuesday	⭐ ⭐	
Wednesday	⭐ ⭐	
Thursday	⭐ ⭐	
Friday	⭐ ⭐	

Spelling Words

scoreboard

outfield

scarecrow

dragonfly

keyboard

undercover

downstairs

anybody

snowflake

southwest

classroom

secondhand

Write about one thing you did each day.

Monday

Tuesday

Wednesday

Thursday

Friday

Keeping Track

Color a book for every 20 minutes you read.

Monday	Tuesday	Wednesday	Thursday	Friday

My favorite book this week was _____.

I liked it because _____

_____

The Peanut

The peanut is one of the most interesting plants in the world. Sometimes known as the "groundnut" or "goober pea," it has many uses. The peanut is not a nut. It belongs to the same family as peas and beans. It has seeds in pods like peas. However, while the pea plant's seedpods grow off its stem, the peanut grows its pods underground.

Peanuts are useful plants. Their seeds are tasty and healthy. Peanut oil is used to oil machinery and to make soap, face powder, shaving cream, shampoo, and paint. Peanut stems and leaves are used in livestock feed and to make fabrics. Even the shells are used to make plastics and wallboard.

The peanut plant is thought to have originated in Brazil or Peru. Portuguese explorers transported it to Africa. From Africa, the peanut was brought to America. Soldiers during the Civil War ate peanuts because they were inexpensive and high in protein.

···

1. What are two other names for peanuts?

   _____   _____

2. Name some of the ways the different parts of a peanut plant are used.

   seed _____

   shell _____

   stem and leaves _____

   oil _____

3. How are peanuts different from the seedpods of peas?

   _____

4. List several different ways that peanuts are eaten.

   _____

   _____

Write It Right

Correct the sentences.

1. to make the pizza crust mr toscano through the doe into the air

   _____

   _____

2. she called shannon her best friend to find out when the picnic will began

   _____

   _____

3. watch out there is broken glass on the floor yelled peter

   _____

   _____

Math Time

Add the following fractions.

1. $\frac{1}{7} + \frac{5}{7} =$ _____

2. $\frac{3}{7} + \frac{3}{7} =$ _____

3. $\frac{1}{6} + \frac{4}{6} =$ _____

Add the following mixed fractions.

4. $1\frac{1}{5} + 2\frac{2}{5} =$ _____

5. $3\frac{1}{4} + 1\frac{2}{4} =$ _____

6. $1\frac{5}{9} + 2\frac{2}{9} =$ _____

Daily Summer Activities • EMC 1075 • © Evan-Moor Corp.

SPELL IT

First draw lines to divide each compound word into syllables. Then write the two words that make up each compound word. Finally, write the number of syllables in each one.

outfield _____ _____ _____

dragonfly _____ _____ _____

anybody _____ _____ _____

keyboard _____ _____ _____

undercover _____ _____ _____

snowflake _____ _____ _____

southwest _____ _____ _____

secondhand _____ _____ _____

Handwriting

Copy these lines from the famous poem *Sea Fever*, by John Masefield.
Use your best handwriting.

I must go down to the seas again, to the lonely sea and the sky. And all I ask is a tall ship and a star to steer her by.

Language Bytes

Add **er** to compare two nouns. Add **est** to compare three or more nouns.
Add **er** or **est** to each of the adjectives to complete the sentences.

1. Lizzie is the fast_____ runner in the class.

2. Tyrone is tall_____ than Syd.

3. The fire alarm is the loud_____ thing I've ever heard.

4. A bratwurst is fatt_____ than a hot dog.

Write a sentence comparing two things.

_____

Write a sentence comparing three or more things.

_____

Math Time

How many containers will you need if…?

4 fish fit in a can	11 fish fit in a box	18 fish fit in a crate

number of fish	cans	boxes	crates
16	4	2	1
9			
25			
37			
45			
75			

George Washington Carver

1860s – 1943

George Washington Carver grew up as an enslaved African American on a plantation in Missouri. As a boy, George loved plants! By the time he was seven or so, people in Diamond Grove, Missouri, called him "The Plant Doctor."

George was a skinny child with a high voice. He stuttered when he talked, but he was determined to learn as much as he could. When he was about ten, he left home to find a town that would allow black children to go to school. He traveled through Missouri and Kansas, going to schools that would accept him, until he graduated from high school. He did laundry to pay his expenses.

In 1890, George began college. He studied art and then agriculture. He was the first black graduate of Iowa State College. Thomas Edison asked George to come to work in his laboratory, but George turned him down. George said that he wanted to help his people. So he set up an agricultural department at Tuskegee Normal School, a new university for black students in Alabama.

George Washington Carver became known as the "Wizard of Tuskegee." His work was instrumental in improving farming in the South. He is especially remembered for his peanut research. He discovered more than 300 uses for the peanut plant.

1. What words would you use to describe George Washington Carver?

_____

_____

2. What makes Dr. Carver's story so inspirational?

_____

_____

_____

```
a  c  s  h  a  m  p  o  o  b  l
s  h  o  e  p  o  l  i  s  h  i
a  o  d  f  h  u  k  n  g  e  n
l  r  u  b  b  e  r  k  m  l  o
a  m  i  p  l  a  s  t  i  c  l
d  y  e  p  e  o  q  s  l  n  e
t  u  s  o  a  p  u  w  k  v  u
x  a  z  i  c  e  c  r  e  a  m
c  e  b  d  h  c  o  f  f  e  e
a  x  l  e  g  r  e  a  s  e  y
```

3. In this word search, find some of the products that Dr. Carver made from peanuts.

Word Box				
salad	rubber	shoe polish	linoleum	milk
coffee	bleach	axle grease	ice cream	soap
dye	ink	shampoo	plastic	

Language Bytes

Homophones are words that sound the same but have different meanings.
Complete each pair of sentences using a pair of homophones from the boxes.

flower
flour

herd
heard

choose
chews

weak
week

1. Mallory _____ the baby crying.

   The _____ of cattle wandered across the fields.

2. I use whole wheat _____ when I make bread.

   She wore a yellow _____ in her hair.

3. Alonzo _____ the gum and then blows a bubble.

   Maria will _____ which frosting to put on the cake.

4. Use the remaining pair of homophones in a sentence.

   _____

Math Time

Find the answers.

1. In the number 26,195, what digit is in

   the thousands place? _____

   the tens place? _____

   the ten-thousands place? _____

   the hundreds place? _____

2. In the number 935,701, what digit is in

   the ones place? _____

   the ten-thousands place? _____

   the tens place? _____

   the hundreds place? _____

3. In the number 6,871,204, what digit is in

   the hundreds place? _____

   the hundred-thousands place? _____

   the millions place? _____

   the ten-thousands place? _____

4. In the number 1,067.4, what digit is in

   the tens place? _____

   the tenths place? _____

   the thousands place? _____

   the ones place? _____

Australia

This graph shows the population of the states and territories of Australia. Use the information to write the population of each state or territory and answer the question.

Western Australia _____

South Australia _____

Queensland _____

Northern Territory _____

New South Wales _____

Victoria _____

Australian
Capital Territory _____

Tasmania _____

How does the population of Victoria compare with the population of South Australia?

_____

_____

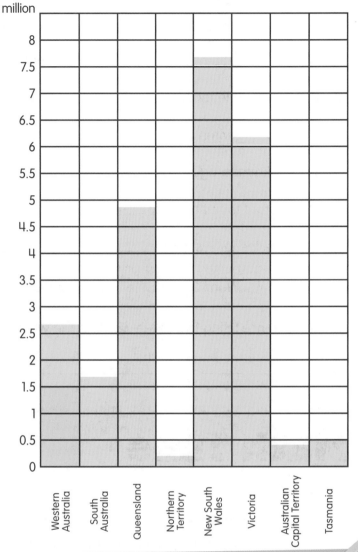

In My Own Words

Summer Is Here!

Write a chant or a cheer for summer. Practice reading it aloud. You may even want to make up actions to go with your words.

Example: Sunny day, sunny day,
Bright, bold, squinty ray,
Sunny day, sunny day,
Let's go out and play.

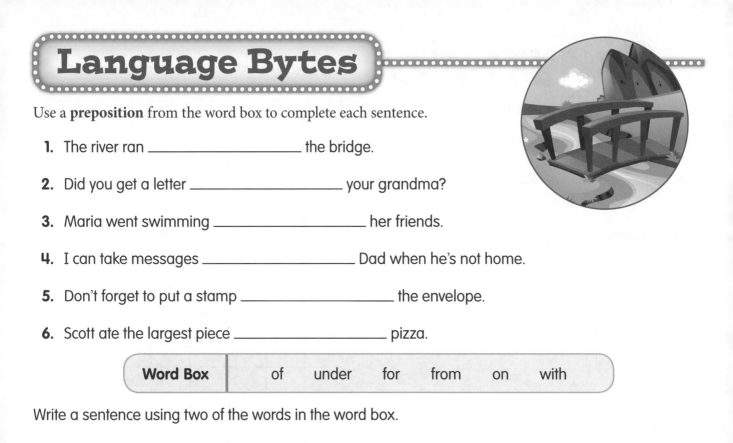

Language Bytes

Use a **preposition** from the word box to complete each sentence.

1. The river ran _____ the bridge.

2. Did you get a letter _____ your grandma?

3. Maria went swimming _____ her friends.

4. I can take messages _____ Dad when he's not home.

5. Don't forget to put a stamp _____ the envelope.

6. Scott ate the largest piece _____ pizza.

Word Box	of under for from on with

Write a sentence using two of the words in the word box.

_____

Math Time

Find the answers.

Work Space

1. Lanie and Fred are each collecting baseball cards.
   If Lanie has three times as many cards as Fred,
   and she has 84, how many cards does Fred have?

   _____

2. Terry has just set up a 10-gallon fish tank in his
   bedroom. He has 10 neon tetras, twice as many
   guppies as tetras, and half as many blue gouramis
   as tetras. How many fish does he have in all?

   _____

3. Matt has 4 pet rats. Eric has 2 parakeets. Kirstin has
   3 gerbils. If each pet eats one-quarter cup of food
   each day, how much food do they need altogether
   for 8 days?

   _____

Write **contractions** to complete the sentences.

_____ going to the park to play. My friend Thomas _____ come with me.
    I am   can not

His mother _____ feeling well, so he will stay home. After _____.
                is not   I have

finished playing, _____ go to the library and check out a book. Then
                       I will

_____ take the book over to Thomas so he _____ feel lonely.
    I will   will not

Math Time

Solve the problems. Then use the key to answer the riddles.

What has eyes but cannot see? _____ _____ _____ _____ _____ _____

662	504	734	426	845	615
−275	−166	−157	−379	−268	−277

What has ears but cannot hear? _____ _____ _____ _____

356	723	783	912
−278	−385	−388	−667

What has a tongue but cannot talk? _____ _____ _____ _____

614	524	836	347
−187	−297	−498	−168

Key	47 = a	227 = h	395 = r	78 = c	245 = n
	179 = e	338 = o	577 = t	387 = p	427 = s

MMMmmm...
Candy Marbles!

Read this recipe for making peanut butter candy.
Follow the directions, and ask an adult to help.

What You Need

$\frac{1}{2}$ cup of chunky peanut butter

$\frac{1}{4}$ cup of evaporated milk

$\frac{1}{4}$ cup of brown sugar

1 teaspoon of cinnamon

1 cup of crispy chow mein noodles, slightly crushed

1 cup of stick pretzels, slightly crushed

$\frac{1}{2}$ cup of chopped nuts

What You Do

1. Stir the peanut butter, evaporated milk, brown sugar, and cinnamon together in a saucepan.

2. Cook over medium heat for five minutes.

3. Remove from heat. Stir in noodles, pretzels, and nuts.

4. Drop spoonfuls onto a foil-lined cookie sheet.

5. Chill for one hour.

6. Pop one in your mouth for a yummy treat!

Daily Summer Activities • EMC 1075 • © Evan-Moor Corp.

Color a ⭐ for each page you finish.

Parent's Initials

Monday ⭐ ⭐

Tuesday ⭐ ⭐

Wednesday ⭐ ⭐

Thursday ⭐ ⭐

Friday ⭐ ⭐

Spelling Words

photograph

alphabet

nephew

enough

cough

half

often

giraffe

officer

whose

clue

refuse

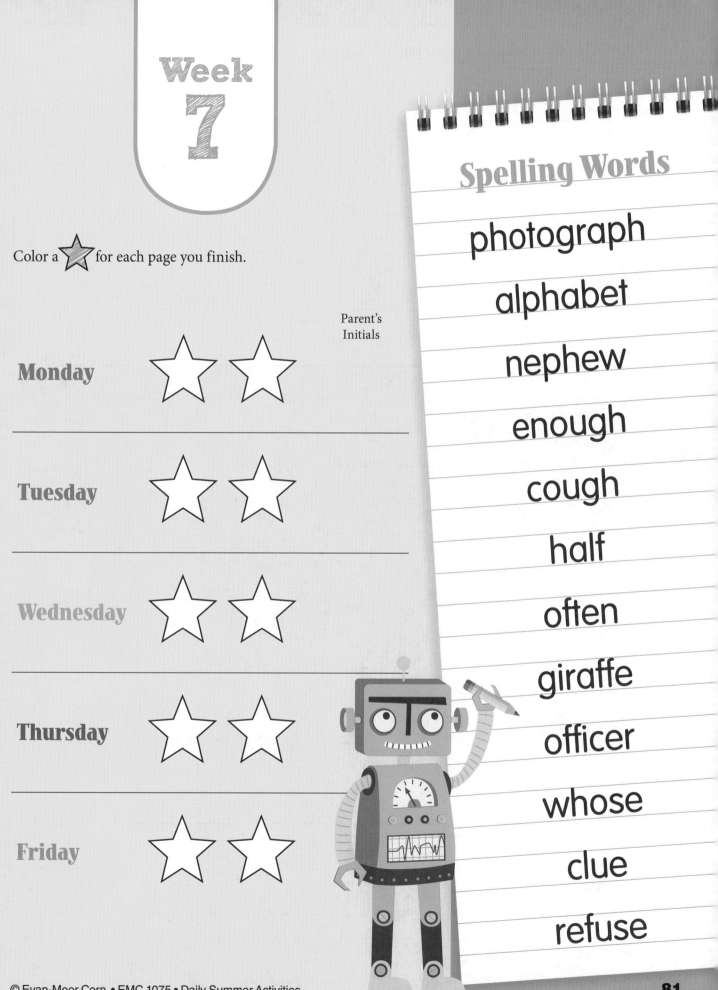

Write about one thing you did each day.

Monday

Tuesday

Wednesday

Thursday

Friday

Keeping Track

Color a book for every 20 minutes you read.

Monday	Tuesday	Wednesday	Thursday	Friday

My favorite book this week was _____.

I liked it because _____

_____.

Jackie Robinson
An Outstanding American

Sometimes a tremendous change can occur as a result of an individual's determination. Jackie Robinson overcame discrimination and segregation to change professional sports forever.

Jackie was a gifted athlete. He was given a scholarship to UCLA. He participated in football, basketball, baseball, and track. Jackie was the first four-sport athlete in the school's history. Despite his success in college, he couldn't play major league professional sports. Sports, like many other areas of American life at that time, were segregated. That meant that players of different races did not play on the same team or against each other.

In 1942, a man named Branch Rickey started managing the Brooklyn Dodgers baseball team. He thought African Americans should be able to play in the major leagues. With the support of the baseball commissioner, the Dodgers' manager asked Jackie Robinson to become a part of his team. He chose Jackie not only for his playing ability, but also for his strong character. Jackie signed a contract in 1945 to play for the Dodgers.

Jackie Robinson excelled in the game. He helped the Dodgers win several pennants and a World Series. He also earned a place in the Baseball Hall of Fame. Jackie Robinson was more than a sports hero; he paved the way in major league sports for other African American athletes.

....

1. What four sports did Jackie participate in during his college career?

    _____ _____ _____ _____

2. The main idea of the story is:

    a. Jackie Robinson was a gifted athlete.

    b. Branch Rickey wanted Jackie Robinson to play in the major leagues.

    c. Jackie Robinson helped to desegregate professional sports.

3. Which words describe Jackie Robinson?

    brave   weak   determined   timid   talented

4. What does **segregated** mean?

    _____

Write It Right

Correct the sentences.

1. the clouds rolled in the sky turned dark and it began to snow

   _____

   _____

2. yes maurice I want you to correct the mistakes on this paper said mr yamaguchi

   _____

   _____

3. cody have drew a diagram of the heart lungs and liver of a mouse

   _____

   _____

Math Time

Find the answers. Show your work.

1. $960 \div 4 =$ _____

2. $917 \div 7 =$ _____

3. $5,498 \div 2 =$ _____

4. $8,580 \div 5 =$ _____

Daily Summer Activities • EMC 1075 • © Evan-Moor Corp.

SPELL IT

Circle the letters in these spelling words that make an **f** sound.

photograph   nephew   cough

alphabet   enough   half

Choose words from the list above to complete the sentences.

1. Uncle Ted has a _____ of me in his wallet. When he says, "That's my

_____ !" it makes me feel good.

2. The letter **z** is not in the first _____ of the _____.

Handwriting

Write the names of the months. Use your best handwriting.

Jumpin' January   *Marvelous May*   *Super September*
Fun-filled February   *Jazzy June*   *Outstanding October*
Magnificent March   *Jolly July*   *Next-to-last November*
Amazing April   *Awesome August*   *Dazzling December*

Language Bytes

Write the correct **abbreviation** for each word.

| qt. | Ave. | lb. | Jr. | St. |
| tbsp. | cm | Mr. | Dr. | ft. |

Avenue _____   Street _____

Mister _____   tablespoon _____

foot _____   Junior _____

pound _____   quart _____

Doctor _____   centimeter _____

Math Time

Find the answers.

Work Space

1. Maurice is three times as tall as his brother. If Maurice is 5 feet, 3 inches tall, how tall is his brother? (Hint: Change Maurice's height to inches.)

   _____

2. Betty has 15 beanbag animals. If she gives $\frac{1}{3}$ of them to her sister, how many will she have left?

   _____

3. Murphy is walking dogs to earn some spending money. If he gets paid $2.50 per dog, and he needs $18.00, how many dogs must he walk?

   _____

The Antarctic Ozone Hole

Ozone is a gas, a form of oxygen. A layer of ozone in the Earth's atmosphere protects Earth and its living things from dangerous ultraviolet radiation in the sun's rays. In 1985, scientists discovered a hole in the ozone layer over Antarctica. The hole is actually a large area with extremely low levels of ozone gas. The low levels usually appear around September and then return to normal by December. However, scientists concluded that pollution from synthetic chemicals was causing the ozone to become thinner. Synthetic chemicals are used in cleaning products, cooling fluid in refrigerators, and aerosol sprays.

In 2006, scientists discovered that the ozone hole was the largest it had ever been, covering 10 million square miles (26 million square km). Since then, the hole has become slightly smaller, and ozone levels have increased, though they are still far below what they were 30 years ago. Despite this short-term improvement, many scientists still fear that the ozone hole could cause damage to the ice, fish, and marine plants in Antarctica.

1. What is the ozone layer?

_____

2. Why is the ozone layer important?

_____

_____

3. What do scientists think is the cause of the ozone hole?

_____

_____

4. What are the possible effects of a decrease in ozone levels?

_____

_____

Language Bytes

Add **commas** to these sentences.

1. Tanya welcome to our class!

2. I can tell Jamal that you've been practicing.

3. I can help you Monday Grandma.

4. Okay Mom. I'm on my way.

5. Sal can you tell me how to do this problem?

6. Hurry up Mark or we're going to be late.

Math Time

Shade the grid to make tenths and hundredths that are equivalent.
Write the missing fractions.

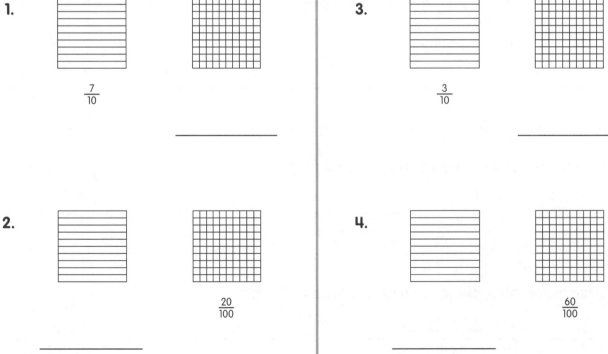

1.

$\frac{7}{10}$

_____

3.

$\frac{3}{10}$

_____

2.

$\frac{20}{100}$

_____

4.

$\frac{60}{100}$

_____

Geography

Name the countries and the bodies of water marked on this map.

A. _____

B. _____

C. _____

D. _____

E. _____

F. _____

G. _____

H. _____

United States, Canada, Mexico, Atlantic Ocean, Pacific Ocean, Gulf of Mexico, Hudson Bay, Bering Sea

In My Own Words   That's Alliteration!

Write three sentences in which every word begins with the same sound.

Begin by trying one with your own name.   Example: Jill jumped John's juniper joyfully.

1. _____

_____

2. _____

_____

3. _____

_____

Language Bytes

Add **commas** to this letter.

> 410 Park Street
> Funville Ohio 43000
> July 30 2000
>
> Dear Pete
>
>   Thank you for the super new shirt. I like the logo the color and the material.
>
> You sure know how to pick out a good present! I hope that you can come to visit soon.
>
> We can go to the zoo have a picnic and see a movie. Thanks again.
>
>   Your pal
>   Fred

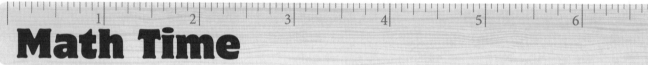

Math Time

Find the answer.

1. What are the common factors of 16 and 24?

   _____

2. What are the first three common multiples of 6 and 8?

   _____

3. Match each number to its set of multiples.

6	10, 15, 20, 25, 30
5	12, 18, 24, 30, 36
8	16, 24, 32, 40, 48

4. Give all the factors of 8.

   _____

Add **quotation marks** to these sentences.

1. How long will the movie last? wondered Tamara.

2. Fernando, will you get the bat? asked Coach Danley.

3. On the way home from the pool, Simon said, I can't wait to warm up!

4. I can't eat spinach, said Fred. I might turn green!

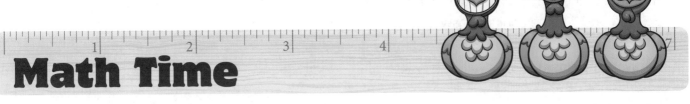

Math Time

As you work on the problem, draw a model if you need to.

Troy needs 3 pounds of blueberries to make a pie. The farm stand has 8 boxes of blueberries. Their weights are shown on the line plot. How many boxes will Troy buy? How much will each box weigh?

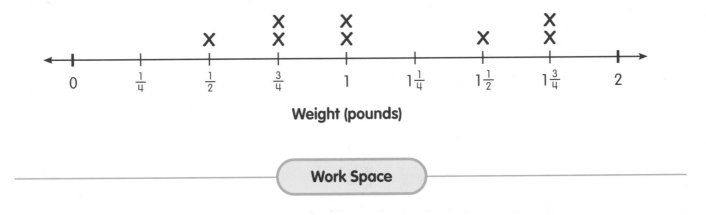

Weight (pounds)

Work Space

Number Puzzle

1. Choose three different digits from 1 to 9.

2. Make the largest and the smallest numbers you can from the three digits.

3. Subtract the smaller number from the larger number.

4. Reverse the order of the digits in the answer, and add it to the original answer.

5. Write the answer.

3, 2, 1

$$\begin{array}{r} 3\,2\,1 \\ -\,1\,2\,3 \\ \hline 1\,9\,8 \\ +\,8\,9\,1 \\ \hline 1{,}089 \end{array}$$

Try it with three digits other than 3, 2, 1.	Try it with four different digits.

How did the answer change from 3 digits to 4 digits?

_____

Do you think the same thing will happen
if you try it with 5 digits?   **Yes   No**

Try it and see.

Daily Summer Activities • EMC 1075 • © Evan-Moor Corp.

Week 8

Color a ⭐ for each page you finish.

Parent's Initials

Monday ☆ ☆

Tuesday ☆ ☆

Wednesday ☆ ☆

Thursday ☆ ☆

Friday ☆ ☆

Spelling Words

truth

due

uniform

future

used

news

voice

noise

disappoint

voyage

loyal

destroy

Write about one thing you did each day.

Monday

_____

Tuesday

_____

Wednesday

_____

Thursday

_____

Friday

Keeping Track

Color a book for every 20 minutes you read.

Monday	Tuesday	Wednesday	Thursday	Friday

My favorite book this week was _____.

I liked it because _____

_____.

Please fill out this application in your best handwriting.

Whatever You Dream Camp

Gymnastics
Baseball
Soccer
Space
Cooking
Science
Music
Horseback Riding

APPLICATION

First Name	Middle Initial	Last Name

( )
Area Code   Telephone

Street Address   City

State   Zip Code

School   Grade

Age   Date of Birth

Full Name of Parent or Guardian

Best Way to Contact Parent or Guardian

If you could go to any kind of camp you wanted, what kind would you choose?

_____

_____

Why would you like to go to this kind of camp?

_____

_____

Write It Right

Correct the sentences.

1. him and me got a reward for finding jeannies lost dog

_____

2. sean had ate popcorn nachos and too hot dogs at the ball game

_____

_____

3. your parents is celebrating there fifteenth anniversary in august

_____

_____

Math Time

Find the answers.

(**Work Space**)

1. The sleepover party ended at 11:45 a.m. If the party lasted 16 hours and 30 minutes, at what time did the party start?

_____

2. Sven can buy a candy bar from the grocery store for 30 cents, but the gas station sells them three for $1.00. Which is the better buy?

_____

3. Diego was traveling about 30 miles per hour while racing his dirt bike. If he kept up this speed for one and one-half hours, about how many miles would he have traveled?

_____

Daily Summer Activities • EMC 1075 • © Evan-Moor Corp.

Fill in the missing letters to write the spelling words.

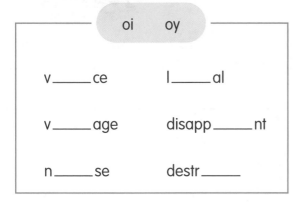

oi	oy
v____ce	l____al
v____age	disapp____nt
n____se	destr____

u	ew	ue
tr____th	n____s
d____	____sed
____niform	f____ture

Write these ice-cream flavors.

rocky road and vanilla
strawberry and bubble gum
butter pecan and chocolate
cookies 'n' cream and lemon sour

_____
- - - - - - - - - - - - - - - - -
_____
_____
- - - - - - - - - - - - - - - - -
_____
_____
- - - - - - - - - - - - - - - - -
_____
_____

What's your favorite flavor? Why?

_____
- - - - - - - - - - - - - - - - -
_____
_____

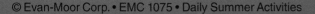

Write It Right

Correct the sentences. Use capital letters where they are needed.

1. jo said that jungle book was her favorite movie.

   _____

   _____

2. my friend joyce lives in evanston illinois.

   _____

   _____

3. dr cook said that i could get my cast off on august 4.

   _____

   _____

Math Time

Find the answers.

51 × 65 = _____   67 × 54 = _____   38 × 72 = _____   24 × 93 = _____

74 × 86 = _____   93 × 24 = _____   48 × 75 = _____   13 × 83 = _____

Colorful Ramblings
from a Crayon Box

"Boy, is it crowded in here! That Jungle Green is in my spot! Will you please move? I wish they would make these boxes bigger!"

"Stop complaining! Soon one of us will be lost or broken, and then there'll be plenty of room."

I listened and observed as the hushed conversation in my crayon box droned on. It was a new 64-color box with a tight lid and bright yellow and green triangles covering its front.

Few crayon users realize that crayons not only speak, but they also have feelings. Just the other day, I witnessed the dismay of a Canary Yellow whose tip was nibbled off by a hungry artist. Have you ever seen the sorrow of a 20-color box that lost its black? Imagine life without a black crayon! You see, crayons have the sensitive souls of artists.

The next time you use a crayon, think about the fragile feelings hidden under the ripped paper covering. Think of the shame and hopelessness in the lost-crayon tub. Take the time to return your crayons to their rightful home. Use them wisely so that their creative potential is realized.

1. From whose point of view is this story being told?

_____

2. What is the purpose of this story?

   a. to give directions

   b. to inform

   c. to entertain

3. The word **droned** means:

   a. to make a loud thump

   b. to make a continous sound

   c. to make a low cry

4. There is a recommendation for crayon users in the story. What is it?

_____

_____

Language Bytes

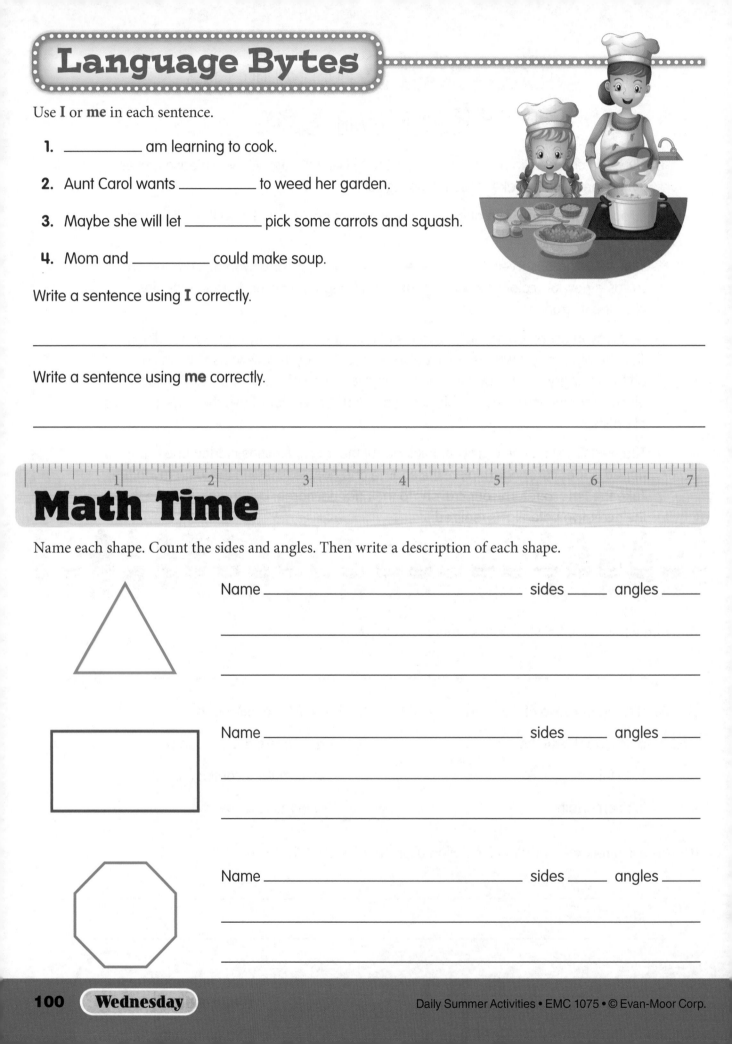

Use **I** or **me** in each sentence.

1. _____ am learning to cook.

2. Aunt Carol wants _____ to weed her garden.

3. Maybe she will let _____ pick some carrots and squash.

4. Mom and _____ could make soup.

Write a sentence using **I** correctly.

_____

Write a sentence using **me** correctly.

_____

Math Time

Name each shape. Count the sides and angles. Then write a description of each shape.

Name _____ sides _____ angles _____

_____

_____

Name _____ sides _____ angles _____

_____

_____

Name _____ sides _____ angles _____

_____

_____

Daily Summer Activities • EMC 1075 • © Evan-Moor Corp.

--Geography

Locate each body of water on this map. Write its letter.

_____ Caribbean Sea

_____ Gulf of California

_____ Arctic Ocean

_____ Great Lakes

_____ Rio Grande

_____ Mississippi River

Color the land green.

In My Own Words

What Animal Are You Like?

Compare yourself to an animal. Tell how you are like that animal and in what ways you are different.

Language Bytes

Complete each sentence using the correct word from the box.
Then circle the words.

1. How _____well_____ did you do?

2. _____ kittens are growing bigger.

3. _____ that boy standing by the pool?

4. Cookies fresh out of the oven taste so _____ .

5. Do you know _____ hat this is?

6. When _____ you going on vacation?

good	well
Are	Our
Who's	Whose
good	well
who's	whose
are	our

Math Time

Subtract the following fractions.

1. $\frac{5}{9} - \frac{1}{9} =$ _____

2. $\frac{6}{7} - \frac{1}{7} =$ _____

3. $\frac{3}{4} - \frac{2}{4} =$ _____

4. $\frac{8}{9} - \frac{1}{9} =$ _____

5. $\frac{4}{5} - \frac{2}{5} =$ _____

Subtract the following mixed fractions.

6. $6\frac{3}{4} - 1\frac{1}{4} =$ _____

7. $5\frac{4}{9} - 1\frac{2}{9} =$ _____

8. $6\frac{6}{7} - 2\frac{1}{7} =$ _____

9. $5\frac{4}{5} - 2\frac{1}{5} =$ _____

10. $8\frac{7}{8} - 5\frac{6}{8} =$ _____

Language Bytes

Circle all the **nouns** in this list.

bake	Trina	school	hospital	long	friend	Tom	pickle
truck	feather	Mr. Gorze	watermelon	funny	Disneyland	park	happy

Write the nouns you circled in the correct category.

Person	**Place**	**Thing**
_____	_____	_____
_____	_____	_____
_____	_____	_____
_____	_____	_____

Math Time

Maria is setting up a lemonade stand. She will sell a glass of lemonade for 20 cents and a cookie for $1.20. Help her complete the chart she will use.

	Price of Lemonade	Price of Cookies	Price of Lemonade + Cookies
1	20¢	$1.20	
2			
3			
4			
5			
6			

Mind Jigglers

Hink Pinks

Hink Pinks are rhyming words that are the answers to clues. For example, an **obese feline** is a **fat cat**. See if you can identify these other hink pinks.

1. an unhappy father: _____

2. a funny young female horse: _____

3. an uncovered seat: _____

4. a contest with fire: _____

5. a hog dance: _____

6. a loyal color: _____

7. not a real cobra: _____

8. a frog relative on the highway: _____

9. a library burglar: _____

10. 24 hours of games: _____

11. a twisted penny: _____

12. an intelligent body organ: _____

13. an orca prison: _____

14. a hilarious rabbit: _____

15. 50 percent of a giggle: _____

16. an ill young chicken: _____

Week 9

Color a ⭐ for each page you finish.

Parent's Initials

Monday ☆ ☆

Tuesday ☆ ☆

Wednesday ☆ ☆

Thursday ☆ ☆

Friday ☆ ☆

Spelling Words

although

together

country

among

cousin

favorite

minute

quarter

several

sure

trouble

which

Write about one thing you did each day.

Monday
_____

Tuesday
_____

Wednesday
_____

Thursday
_____

Friday

Keeping Track

Color a book for every 20 minutes you read.

Monday	Tuesday	Wednesday	Thursday	Friday

My favorite book this week was _____.

I liked it because _____

_____.

--Geography

Using this map, give specific directions for traveling from the Oxley Nature Center to the Philbrook Museum of Art.

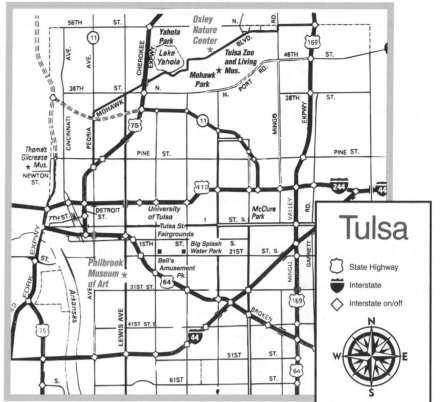

_____

_____

_____

_____

_____

_____

In My Own Words   Impossible!

Write about something people thought was impossible in the past.

Write about something you did that you thought was impossible.

Write about something you think is impossible now but might be possible in the future.

Language Bytes

Use **can** or **may** in each sentence.

1. _____ I please go to Tori's party?

2. Chelsea runs so fast, she _____ always score a goal.

3. Yvette _____ make a birdhouse without any help.

4. I _____ carry all the groceries inside.

5. You _____ not bring your radio to the dinner table.

Write a sentence using **can**.

_____

Write a sentence using **may**.

_____

Math Time

Choose the correct answer.

1. A baby weighed 8 lb., 3 oz. at birth. At age 3 months, the baby weighed 12 lb., 5 oz. How much weight did the baby gain in three months?

   a. 4 lb., 2 oz.   **b.** 5 lb.   **c.** 4 lb., 9 oz.

2. The wheelbarrow weighed 30 kilograms when it was full of sand. When empty it weighed 12 kilograms, 25 grams. How much sand does it hold?

   a. 18 kilograms   **b.** 17 kilograms, 75 grams   **c.** 17 kilograms, 975 grams

3. The recipe calls for 3 cups of juice to make enough punch for 6 people. How much juice is needed to make punch for one dozen people?

   a. 5 cups   **b.** 1 quart, 2 cups   **c.** 1 quart, 3 cups

Language Bytes

Complete each sentence using the correct word. Then circle the word.

1. They _____ the game carefully.

2. Mystery stories _____ exciting.

3. My hen _____ eggs in the nest.

4. The girls _____ beautifully.

play	plays
is	are
lay	lays
dance	dances

Write a sentence about a **helicopter**.

_____

Write a sentence about **four snails**.

_____

Math Time

Find the answers.

1. How many feet are in three yards?

   _____

2. How many centimeters are in two meters?

   _____

3. How many inches are in one yard?

   _____

4. How many meters are in two and a half kilometers?

   _____

Analogies

In an **analogy**, each pair of items has the same relationship.

Bird is to **sky** as **fish** is to **sea**.

Here is a shorter way to write an analogy.

bird : **sky** :: **fish** : **sea**

Choose the correct word to complete the analogy.

1. **Wall** is to **brick** as **skeleton** is to _____.

    foot, legs, bone, skin

2. **Sail** is to **boat** as **engine** is to _____.

    truck, battery, drive, bicycle

3. **Hand** is to **mitten** as **head** is to _____.

    arm, coat, hat, hair

4. **tall** : **short** :: **night** : _____

    twilight, dark, long, day

5. **flashlight** : **light** :: **furnace** : _____

    ice, winter, night, heat

6. **camel** : **desert** :: **ship** : _____

    sand, vehicle, ocean, passenger

Analogies...

7. **closet** : **clothes** :: **refrigerator** : _____

    house, food, ice cream, kitchen

Write two analogies of your own.

_____ : _____ :: _____ : _____

_____ : _____ :: _____ : _____

Week 10

Color a ★ for each page you finish.

Parent's Initials

Monday ★★

Tuesday ★★

Wednesday ★★

Thursday ★★

Friday ★★

Spelling Words

happiness

worthless

useless

smartest

kindest

largest

fearful

harmful

cheerful

quickly

suddenly

busiest

Write about one thing you did each day.

Monday

_____

Tuesday

_____

Wednesday

_____

Thursday

_____

Friday

Keeping Track

Color a book for every 20 minutes you read.

Monday	Tuesday	Wednesday	Thursday	Friday

My favorite book this week was _____.

I liked it because _____

_____.

Farming with Worms

Worms are good composters. They eat organic waste and turn it into soil. Start your own worm farm, and soon you will reduce the amount of organic trash that you throw away.

Your worm farm container should be about the size of a bag of groceries. Experienced worm farmers believe that wood makes the best worm farm container. Drill holes in the bottom of the container for drainage and air circulation. Make one hole every 3 to 4 inches. Set the container on bricks so the air can get into the box through the holes. Your container will need a plastic cover just a little smaller than the top of the container.

Tear old newspaper into strips about an inch wide. Soak the newspaper strips in water until they are soggy. Put a layer of soggy strips in the box. Add several handfuls of soil and mix. Your farm is ready for worms. Add a pound of red wigglers. (That's about 1,000 worms!) You can buy them at a feed store or a bait shop.

In a few days, you will need to feed your worms. Lift the plastic cover. Add a few scraps of food. Cover the scraps with 2 to 3 inches of soggy newspaper strips. Put the plastic top back in place.

Your worm farm is a miniature compost pile.

....

1. Why are worm farms valuable?

   _____

   _____

2. What materials are needed to build a worm farm?

   _____

   _____

3. What does "Worms are good composters" mean?

   _____

4. What evidence can you find in the story to support the idea that worms don't weigh very much?

   _____

Write It Right

Correct the sentences.

1. did you see the rattlesnake special on pbs i seen it twice

   _____

   _____

2. me and my family is visiting orlando florida for an week said dr luiz

   _____

   _____

3. the coach selected marco my oldest brother two be her helper

   _____

   _____

Math Time

Find the answer. Explain how you figured it out.

Eric was looking in the refrigerator and saw two pitchers of punch. He wanted to combine them into a single 2-quart pitcher, but he didn't know if the pitcher was big enough. The first small pitcher held 1 quart, and it was half full. The other pitcher held 2 quarts, and it was about three-fourths full. Could Eric pour the remaining punch from the smaller pitcher into the larger one without overflowing the pitcher?

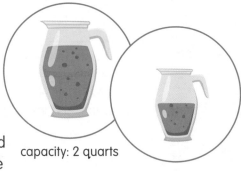

capacity: 2 quarts

capacity: 1 quart

   _____

   _____

   _____

SPELL IT

What **suffixes** could you use?

> ful ly est less

1. use   _____ _____
2. quick   _____ _____
3. busy   _____ _____
4. large   _____ _____
5. worth   _____

6. cheer   _____ _____
7. harm   _____ _____
8. smart   _____ _____
9. kind   _____ _____

Handwriting

Copy this paragraph in your best handwriting.

Hot sun warms the Earth and causes water to evaporate. When the water vapor rises up into the sky, it meets cold air and condenses into droplets. Millions of drops join to make clouds. When a cloud is full, raindrops fall back to Earth.

Language Bytes

Add **es** to each verb. You may have to change **y** to **i** first.

rush_____   fry_____   mix_____   buzz_____

Write the correct verb to complete each sentence.

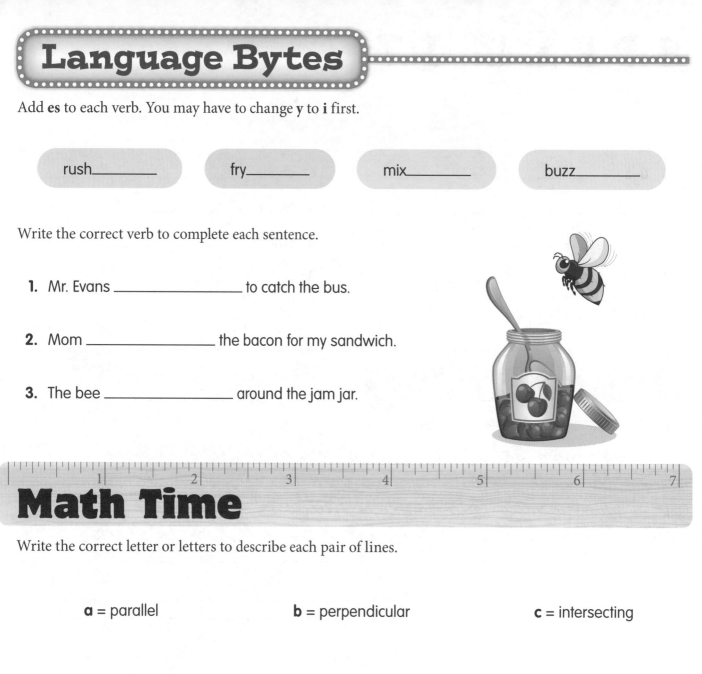

1. Mr. Evans _____ to catch the bus.

2. Mom _____ the bacon for my sandwich.

3. The bee _____ around the jam jar.

Math Time

Write the correct letter or letters to describe each pair of lines.

a = parallel   **b** = perpendicular   **c** = intersecting

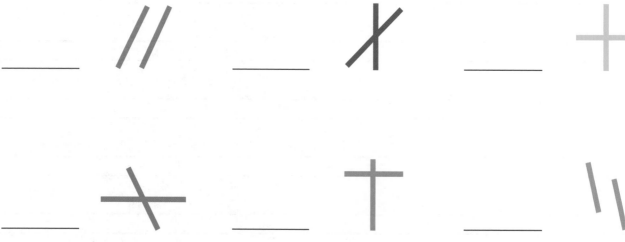

The Farming Business

In many parts of the world, farming is a very big business. Farmers need to know much more than how to plant a seed. They need to know how to plan ahead, how machines work, what soil conditions make plants grow well, and how to keep track of money.

To plan their farming year, farmers must know what crops people will buy. They study government reports and other materials to decide what to grow each year.

Some crops require specific kinds of machines to plant, cultivate, or harvest them. The farmer must decide which machines to buy or rent each year. The machinery is purchased or rented with the money from last year's crops.

Some crops require special kinds of soil to grow well. The farmer must study the chemistry of the soil and plan how to make the soil best for the crops. Sometimes fertilizer or chemicals must be purchased to improve the soil.

All this planning requires money. The farmer must keep close track of the money earned by selling the crops. Each year money must be spent on machinery, soil conditioners, and, of course, seed. The farmer must be a good money manager to have a successful farm.

A farmer must combine knowledge of many different occupations to be successful. Explain how a farmer is like:

a scientist _____

_____

a mechanic _____

_____

a fortune-teller _____

_____

a weather forecaster _____

_____

an accountant _____

_____

Language Bytes

An **adverb** tells how, when, or where.

Circle the adverb that tells about each underlined verb.
Then write **how**, **when**, or **where** to tell how the adverb is used.

1. Annie <u>sang</u> quietly to her little sister. _____

2. Carlos <u>practiced</u> ball yesterday. _____

3. When I dropped the box, the cereal <u>flew</u> everywhere. _____

4. The boy <u>waited</u> patiently for his turn. _____

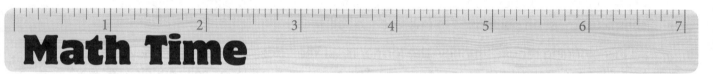

Math Time

Write the answers.

1. Label each angle: **right**, **obtuse**, **acute**.

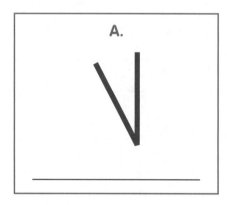

A.

_____

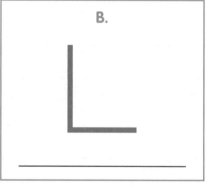

B.

_____

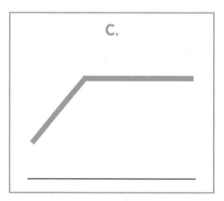

C.

_____

2. Choose the best estimate for each angle.

   A. 30° 60° 70° 100° _____

   B. 20° 45° 90° 140° _____

   C. 60° 95° 120° 180° _____

3. How could you check your estimates? _____

Answer Key

Checking your child's work is an important part of learning. It allows you to see what your child knows well and what areas need more practice. It also provides an opportunity for you to help your child understand that making mistakes is a part of learning.

When an error is discovered, ask your child to look carefully at the question or problem. Errors often occur through misreading the problem. Your child can quickly correct these errors.

The answer key pages can be used in several ways:

- Remove the answer pages and give the book to your child. Go over the answers with him or her as each day's work is completed.

- Leave the answer pages in the book and give the practice pages to your child one day at a time.

- Leave the answer pages in the book so your child can check his or her own answers as the pages are completed. It is still important that you review the pages with your child if you use this method.

Page 11

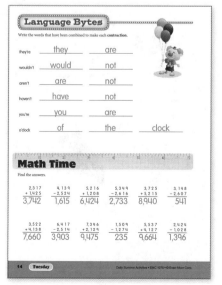

Introducing the Spotted Salamander

The spotted salamander remains almost unchanged from the first salamander that walked on the Earth about 300 million years ago. It lives in caves or under rocks and logs, and it moves only during the blackest hours of the night. It eats insects and worms and lives in the earthen darkness, just as its early ancestors did. Its soft legs, clawless toes, and moist body look just like those of generations of salamanders that have come before it.

Its eyes peer into the darkness, but they do not move like other creatures' eyes. The spotted salamander sees only things that move. It cannot see things that are still. It "hears" with primitive ears that lie inside its head and along its body and tail.

Once a year, on the night of the first spring rain after the first spring thaw, it visits the same woodland pond that its ancestors visited. There it lays its eggs. Then it returns to the darkness of its home in the moist earth of the forest.

1. What is the main idea of this article?
   The spotted salamander has changed little in millions of years.
2. List three supporting details that tell about the main idea.
   body looks like salamander of past
   diet and habitat same as ancestors'
   has primitive eyes and ears

3. Underline the topic sentence in the first paragraph.

4. How are the eyes and ears of the spotted salamander different from those of most animals today?
   Its eyes do not move and see only movement. Besides being inside its head, its ears lie along its body/tail.

Monday Week 1 11

Page 12

Write It Right

Correct the sentences.

1. in april we will have cheerleading tryouts at lincoln junior high
   In April, we will have cheerleading tryouts at Lincoln Junior High.

2. tonya slip on the ice she fall on her write foot
   Tonya slipped on the ice. She fell on her right foot. OR Tonya slipped on the ice and fell on her right foot.

3. mrs jackson mrs ruiz and mr evans is in charge of the basketball team
   Mrs. Jackson, Mrs. Ruiz, and Mr. Evans are in charge of the basketball team.

Math Time

Write the place value of the 4 in the numbers below.

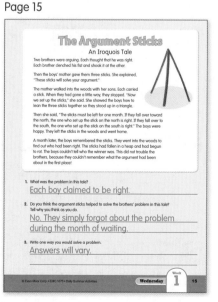

4,093	4 thousands
$14.92	4 ones (dollars)
948	4 tens
74	4 ones
8.4	4 tenths
42,081	4 ten thousands
6.04	4 hundredths
4,982,000	4 millions

12 Monday

Page 13

S P E L L   I T

R controls many vowel sounds so that the **vowel + r** makes the sound you hear in words like **her**. Underline the r-controlled vowel sounds in these words.

world   doctor   learn   thirsty   danger   purchase

Use the words above to complete these sentences.

1. There are many places in the ___world___ where people are ___thirsty___ because there is not enough water.

2. The ___doctor___ warned her patient about the ___danger___ of the operation.

3. It is important to ___learn___ about the features of an automobile before you ___purchase___ it.

Handwriting

Copy this riddle in your best handwriting. Then answer it.

'Round and 'round the rugged rock
the ragged rascal ran.
How many R's are there in that?
Now tell me if you can.

Answer: There are no r's in "that."

Round and 'round the rugged rock
the ragged rascal ran.
How many R's are there in that?
Now tell me if you can.

Tuesday Week 1 13

Page 14

Language Bytes

Write the words that have been combined to make each contraction.

they're	they	are
wouldn't	would	not
aren't	are	not
haven't	have	not
you're	you	are
o'clock	of	the	clock

Math Time

Find the answers.

2,317 +1,425 = **3,742**	4,139 −2,524 = **1,615**	5,216 +1,208 = **6,424**	5,349 −2,616 = **2,733**	3,725 +5,215 = **8,940**	3,148 −2,607 = **541**
3,522 +4,138 = **7,660**	6,417 −2,514 = **3,903**	7,346 +2,129 = **9,475**	1,509 −1,274 = **235**	5,537 +4,127 = **9,664**	2,424 −1,028 = **1,396**

14 Tuesday

Page 15

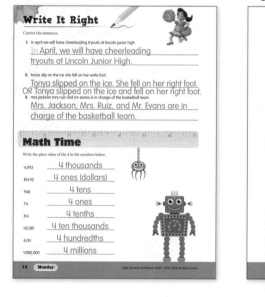

The Argument Sticks
An Iroquois Tale

Two brothers were arguing. Each thought that he was right. Each brother clenched his fist and shook it at the other.

Then the boys' mother gave them three sticks. She explained, "These sticks will solve your argument."

The mother walked into the woods with her sons. Each carried a stick. When they had gone a little way, they stopped. "Now we set up the sticks," she said. She showed the boys how to lean the three sticks together so they stood up in a triangle.

Then she said, "The sticks must be left for one month. If they fall over toward the north, the one who set up the stick on the north is right. If they fall over to the south, the one who set up the stick on the south is right." The boys were happy. They left the sticks in the woods and went home.

A month later, the boys remembered the sticks. They went into the woods to find out who had been right. The sticks had fallen in a heap and had begun to rot. The boys couldn't tell who the winner was. This did not trouble the brothers, because they couldn't remember what the argument had been about in the first place!

1. What was the problem in this tale?
   Each boy claimed to be right.

2. Do you think the argument sticks helped to solve the brothers' problem in this tale? Tell why you think so.
   No. They simply forgot about the problem during the month of waiting.

3. Write one way you would solve a problem.
   Answers will vary.

Wednesday Week 1 15

Page 16

Language Bytes

Write definitions of the underlined word or words. Use the **context** (the meaning of the sentence) to help you. Then check your definition with a dictionary or other resource.

1. The spotted salamander is active at night, so we call it nocturnal.
   active at night

2. The descendants of the first spotted salamander haven't changed significantly in over 300 million years.
   family members that come later in time

3. From deep in the cave, the spelunker peered up through the crevice in the rocks.
   cave explorer   a crack or opening

4. He knew it would be difficult to traverse the slick walls of the cave, but he needed to get to the other side.
   move across

Math Time

A **ratio** is a special comparison of two numbers. Express the ratios shown below.

Write how many shaded squares and how many white squares are in each row.

4 , 2	What is the ratio of shaded squares to white squares for the whole figure?
3 , 3	15:15 or 1:1
3 , 3	Were you surprised at the overall ratio? Tell why or why not.
1 , 5	Answers will
4 , 2	vary.

16 Wednesday

© Evan-Moor Corp. • EMC 1075 • Daily Summer Activities

Page 17

Geography

The globe can be divided in half two ways. Each half is called a **hemisphere**. When the globe is divided at the equator, the Southern and Northern Hemispheres are created. When it is divided along 0° longitude and 180° longitude, the Western and Eastern Hemispheres are created.

Use the drawings to identify the hemispheres in which you live. Then complete the sentences.

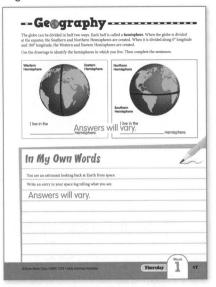

Western Hemisphere | Eastern Hemisphere

Northern Hemisphere | Southern Hemisphere

I live in the _____ Hemisphere.
I live in the _____ Hemisphere.

Answers will vary.

In My Own Words

You are an astronaut looking back at Earth from space.

Write an entry in your space log telling what you see.

Answers will vary.

Thursday • Week 1 • 17

Page 18

Language Bytes

A **noun** names a person, place, or thing.
Circle the nouns in the passage below.

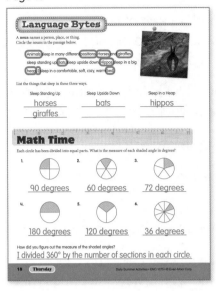

(Animals) sleep in many different positions. (Horses) and (giraffes) sleep standing up. (Bats) sleep upside down. (Hippos) sleep in a big (heap.) (I) sleep in a comfortable, soft, cozy, warm (bed.)

List the things that sleep in these three ways.

Sleep Standing Up	Sleep Upside Down	Sleep in a Heap
horses	bats	hippos
giraffes		

Math Time

Each circle has been divided into equal parts. What is the measure of each shaded angle in degrees?

1. **90 degrees**
2. **60 degrees**
3. **72 degrees**
4. **180 degrees**
5. **120 degrees**
6. **36 degrees**

How did you figure out the measure of the shaded angles?

I divided 360° by the number of sections in each circle.

18 • Thursday

Page 19

Language Bytes

Write these words in alphabetical order.

turn, duck, whistle, eagle, Relax!, hawk, zip, juniper, lupine, Nice!, grouse, yell, maple, Perfect!, apples, Quiet!, falcon, ivy, Shush!, bananas, unpack, vote, cherries, Ouch!, kudzu

apples	falcon	kudzu	Perfect!	unpack
bananas	grouse	lupine	Quiet!	vote
cherries	hawk	maple	Relax!	whistle
duck	ivy	Nice!	Shush!	yell
eagle	juniper	Ouch!	turn	zip

The list above can be divided into five categories. Color the boxes in each category a different color.

Math Time

Find the answers.

1. Thomas is saving money to buy a video game. The game costs $24.95. If he has $12.50, how much more money does Thomas need?

   24.95 – 12.50 = $12.45

2. Sally's dog had six puppies. If Sally keeps one puppy for herself and sells the others for $12 each, how much money will she earn?

   5 × 12 = $60

3. Dave has five more chickens than he has dogs. He has one less cat than he has dogs. If he has three dogs, how many pets does he have?

   3 + 8 + 2 = 13 pets

Work Space
Work will vary.

Friday • Week 1 • 19

Page 20

Whose Tree?

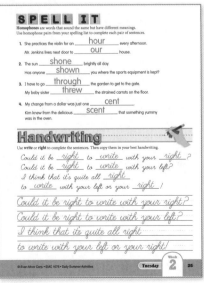

The people in each U.S. state have chosen a tree to represent their state. Use the clues and the matrix to match the following states and their trees. Write **yes** to show a correct answer. Make an **X** to show incorrect answers.

- Rhode Island's tree is two words. The first letter of the first word for the state and the tree are the same.
- California's tree is named for the color of its trunk.
- The American elm is not the state tree of Florida, Nevada, or Georgia.
- Oregon's tree is a popular Christmas tree that begins with a person's name.
- The name of South Carolina's tree begins with the same letter as the state.
- The single-leaf piñon tree represents a state that borders California.

	redwood	single-leaf piñon	American elm	live oak	Douglas fir	Sabal palmetto	red maple
Oregon	X	X	X	X	yes	X	X
Massachusetts and N. Dakota	X	X	yes	X	X	X	X
Rhode Island	X	X	X	X	X	X	yes
California	yes	X	X	X	X	X	X
Florida and S. Carolina	X	X	X	X	X	yes	X
Nevada	X	yes	X	X	X	X	X
Georgia	X	X	X	yes	X	X	X

20 • Friday

Page 23

Jesse Owens

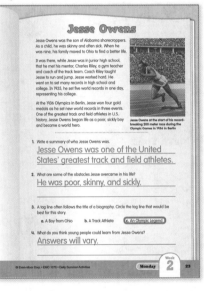

Jesse Owens was the son of Alabama sharecroppers. As a child, he was skinny and often sick. When he was nine, his family moved to Ohio to find a better life.

It was there, while Jesse was in junior high school, that he met his mentor, Charles Riley, a gym teacher and coach of the track team. Coach Riley taught Jesse to run and jump. Jesse worked hard. He went on to set many records in high school and college. In 1935, he set five world records in one day, representing his college.

At the 1936 Olympics in Berlin, Jesse won four gold medals as he set new world records in three events. One of the greatest track and field athletes in U.S. history, Jesse Owens began life as a poor, sickly boy and became a world hero.

Jesse Owens at the start of his record-breaking 200 meter race during the Olympic Games in 1936 in Berlin

1. Write a summary of who Jesse Owens was.
   Jesse Owens was one of the United States' greatest track and field athletes.

2. What are some of the obstacles Jesse overcame in his life?
   He was poor, skinny, and sickly.

3. A tag line often follows the title of a biography. Circle the tag line that would be best for this story.
   a. A Boy from Ohio   b. A Track Athlete   (c. An Olympic Legend)

4. What do you think young people could learn from Jesse Owens?
   Answers will vary.

Monday • Week 2 • 23

Page 24

Write It Right

Correct the sentences.

1. mom said we needs to stop to bye gas before we leave to bass lake
   Mom said, "We need to stop to buy gas before we leave for Bass Lake."

2. ben taked pictures of the team for boy's life magazine
   Ben took pictures of the team for Boy's Life magazine.

3. does you like a aluminum bat or an wooden one
   Do you like an aluminum bat or a wooden one?

Math Time

Find the answers.

805 −102 **703**	750 −230 **520**	620 −420 **200**	279 −180 **99**	530 −267 **263**
497 −359 **138**	549 −524 **25**	725 −225 **500**	737 −638 **99**	462 −421 **41**
4,591 − 442 **4,149**	2,985 −2,765 **220**	5,900 −1,648 **4,252**	53,986 −28,999 **24,987**	766,533 −445,624 **320,909**

24 • Monday

Page 25

SPELL IT

Homophones are words that sound the same but have different meanings.
Use homophone pairs from your spelling list to complete each pair of sentences.

1. She practices the violin for an **hour** every afternoon.
   Mr. Jenkins lives next door to **our** house.

2. The sun **shone** brightly all day.
   Has anyone **shown** you where the sports equipment is kept?

3. I have to go **through** the garden to get to the gate.
   My baby sister **threw** the strained carrots on the floor.

4. My change from a dollar was just one **cent**.
   Kim knew from the delicious **scent** that something yummy was in the oven.

Handwriting

Use **write** or **right** to complete the sentences. Then copy them in your best handwriting.

Could it be **right** to **write** with your **right**?
Could it be **right** to **write** with your left?
I think that it's quite all **right**
to **write** with your left or your **right**!

Could it be right to write with your right?
Could it be right to write with your left?
I think that it's quite all right
to write with your left or your right!

Tuesday • Week 2 • 25

Page 26

Language Bytes

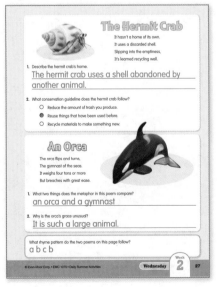

Write **a** or **an** in front of each noun below.

an armadillo   **a** mountain
an icicle   **a** dragonfly
an eagle   **a** garage
a zipper   **an** obstacle

Write a sentence that explains when you use **a** and when you use **an** before a noun.

Use "an" before nouns that begin with a vowel sound, and use "a" before the others.

Math Time

Measure the lines in inches.

AB is **1 3/4 inches**
BC is **3 inches**
AC is **2 1/4 inches**

AB + AC is longer than BC.
(yes)   no

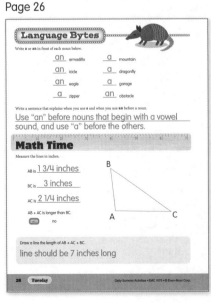

Draw a line the length of AB + AC + BC.

line should be 7 inches long

26 • Tuesday

Page 27

The Hermit Crab

It hasn't a home of its own.
It uses a discarded shell.
Slipping into the emptiness,
It's learned recycling well.

1. Describe the hermit crab's home.
   The hermit crab uses a shell abandoned by another animal.

2. What conservation guideline does the hermit crab follow?
   ○ Reduce the amount of trash you produce.
   ● Reuse things that have been used before.
   ○ Recycle materials to make something new.

An Orca

The orca flips and turns,
The gymnast of the seas.
It weighs four tons or more
But breaches with great ease.

1. What two things does the metaphor in this poem compare?
   an orca and a gymnast

2. Why is the orca's grace unusual?
   It is such a large animal.

What rhyme pattern do the two poems on this page follow?
a b c b

Wednesday • Week 2 • 27

Page 28

Language Bytes

1. A yard is a measurement of length. What else can the word **yard** mean?
the area around a home

Write one sentence using the two different meanings of the word **yard**.
Sentences will vary.

2. A key is a metal object used to turn the bolt of a lock.
What does the word **key** mean in this sentence?
The map key indicates that the city has an airport.
A map key explains the symbols used on the map.

Math Time
Find the answers.

Work Space

1. Ivan likes ice cream from Mr. Sweet's ice-cream parlor. A single scoop costs $1.25, and a double scoop costs $2. If Ivan's grandfather pays him 50 cents an hour when he works in the garden, how many hours will Ivan have to work to buy a single scoop? A double scoop?
3 hours single
4 hours double

2. Mr. Sweet can make 40 single-scoop cones from a five-gallon tub of ice cream. If the tub of ice cream and the cones cost $28, what is Mr. Sweet's profit if he sells only single scoops?
$22 profit

Work will vary.
1.25 ÷ .50 = 2.5
2.00 ÷ .50 = 4

1.25 × 40 = 50
50 − 28 = 22

Wednesday 28

Page 29

Geography
Match the word with the phrase that tells what it means.

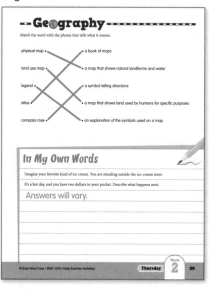

physical map — a book of maps
land use map — a map that shows natural landforms and water
legend — a symbol telling directions
atlas — a map that shows land used by humans for specific purposes
compass rose — an explanation of the symbols used on a map

In My Own Words
Imagine your favorite kind of ice cream. You are standing outside the ice-cream store.
It's a hot day, and you have two dollars in your pocket. Describe what happens next.
Answers will vary.

Thursday Week 2 29

Page 30

Language Bytes
The underlined phrase in each sentence is an idiom. It has a special, nonliteral meaning. Write the meaning of each idiom.

1. Johnny was horsing around.
being playful, goofing around

2. Tommy is always on the ball.
alert, paying attention, quick to respond

3. Mr. Jones's bark is worse than his bite.
sounds mean or angry, but really isn't

Math Time
Find the answers.

308 × 7 = **2,156**	769 × 4 = **3,076**	853 × 6 = **5,118**	972 × 9 = **8,748**
657 × 1 = **657**	896 × 8 = **7,168**	409 × 8 = **3,272**	892 × 6 = **5,352**
738 × 0 = **0**	557 × 9 = **5,013**	985 × 5 = **4,925**	850 × 7 = **5,950**

Thursday 30

Page 31

Language Bytes
The answer to each question is a pair of rhyming words. The first word of each rhyming pair is in the word box. Find the other word in the rhyming pair, and write the answer to the question on the line.

Word Box red big flat green lucky marriage

1. What do you call someone whose hair is the color of a tomato? **redhead**
2. What do you call a large hog? **big pig**
3. What do you call a cap after an elephant sits on it? **flat hat**
4. What do you call a grass-colored vegetable? **green bean**
5. What do you call a web-footed winner? **lucky ducky**
6. What do you call a wagon used by the bride and groom? **marriage carriage**

Math Time
Pete collects bugs and keeps them in a box. Once a week he opens the lid to add 5 new bugs. Each time he does, 3 bugs get away. If he starts with 18 bugs, how many bugs will he have at the end of six weeks? Complete this table to find the answer to the question.
Answer: **30**

	Week 1	Week 2	Week 3	Week 4	Week 5	Week 6
Beginning of Week	18	20	22	24	26	28
Bugs In	5	5	5	5	5	5
Bugs Out	3	3	3	3	3	3
End of Week	20	22	24	26	28	30

Friday Week 2 31

Page 32

Magic Squares
Fill in each magic square. Use the numerals 1 through 9. Use each number only once. The numbers must total 15 when they are added together horizontally and vertically per square. Give three different solutions.

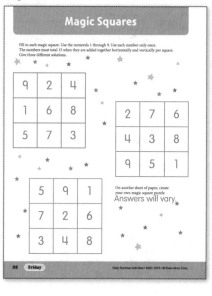
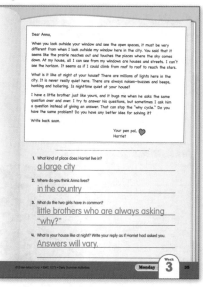

9	2	4
1	6	8
5	7	3

2	7	6
4	3	8
9	5	1

5	9	1
7	2	6
3	4	8

On another sheet of paper, create your own magic square puzzle.
Answers will vary.

Friday 32

Page 35

Dear Anna,

When you look outside your window and see the open spaces, it must be very different from when I look outside my window here in the city. You said that it seems like the prairie reaches out and touches the places where the sky comes down. At my house, all I can see from my windows are houses and streets. I can't see the horizon. It seems as if I could climb from roof to roof to reach the stars.

What is it like at night at your house? There are millions of lights here in the city. It is never really quiet here. There are always noises—buzzes and beeps, honking and hollering. Is nighttime quiet at your house?

I have a little brother just like yours, and it bugs me when he asks the same question over and over. I try to answer his questions, but sometimes I ask him a question instead of giving an answer. That can stop the "why cycle." Do you have the same problem? Do you have any better idea for solving it?

Write back soon.

Your pen pal,
Harriet

1. What kind of place does Harriet live in?
a large city

2. Where do you think Anna lives?
in the country

3. What do the two girls have in common?
little brothers who are always asking "why?"

4. What is your house like at night? Write your reply as if Harriet had asked you.
Answers will vary.

Monday Week 3 35

Page 36

Write It Right
Correct the sentences.

1. clarise antonio and margaret have went to tennis camp since they was seven
Clarise, Antonio, and Margaret have gone to tennis camp since they were seven.

2. morris leaved his job and moved to dallas texas to be a fire fighter
Morris left his job and moved to Dallas, Texas, to be a firefighter.

3. the scientists didnt gave up when they couldnt figure out the problem
The scientists didn't give up when they couldn't figure out the problem.

Math Time
Find the area and the perimeter.

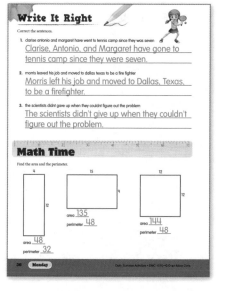

area **135**
perimeter **48**

area **144**
perimeter **48**

area **48**
perimeter **32**

Monday 36

Page 37

SPELL IT
Write the two words that make up the compound word. Then explain the meaning of the compound word by writing a sentence that uses the word.
breakfast   break + fast
You break your nightlong fast when you eat breakfast.

1. earthquake   **earth** + **quake**
Sentences will vary.
2. headache   **head** + **ache**
3. lifeguard   **life** + **guard**
4. applesauce   **apple** + **sauce**

Handwriting

Copy these words.
skyscraper
everywhere
skyscraper
everywhere

Copy these words.
Yolanda
yesterday
Yolanda
yesterday

Tuesday Week 3 37

Page 38

Language Bytes
Use a conjunction (and, but, or) to combine each pair of simple sentences into a compound sentence. Use a comma before each conjunction.

1. Aunt Carol baked cookies. The children ate them all.
Aunt Carol baked cookies, and the children ate them all.

2. The explorers searched the ice field. They never reached the South Pole.
The explorers searched the ice field, but they never reached the South Pole.

3. Jana might walk to the park with us. Maybe she will meet us there.
Jana might walk to the park with us, or maybe she will meet us there.

Math Time
Find the answers.

$\frac{1}{2} + \frac{1}{2} = \frac{2}{2}$ $\frac{1}{8} + \frac{5}{8} = \frac{6}{8}$ $\frac{2}{4} + \frac{1}{4} = \frac{3}{4}$

$\frac{2}{6} + \frac{1}{6} = \frac{4}{6}$ $\frac{1}{3} + \frac{2}{3} = \frac{3}{3}$ $\frac{6}{12} + \frac{1}{12} = \frac{7}{12}$

Tuesday 38

Page 39

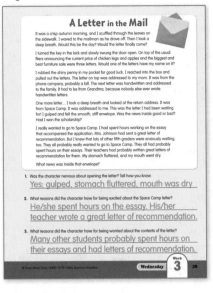

A Letter in the Mail

It was a crisp autumn morning, and I scuffled through the leaves on the sidewalk. I waved to the mailman as he drove off. Then I took a deep breath. Would this be the day? Would the letter finally come?

I turned the key in the lock and slowly swung the door open. On top of the usual fliers announcing the current price of chicken legs and apples and the biggest and best furniture sale were three letters. Would one of the letters have my name on it?

I rubbed the shiny penny in my pocket for good luck. I reached into the box and pulled out the letters. The letter on top was addressed to my mom. It was from the phone company, probably a bill. The next letter was handwritten and addressed to the family. It had to be from Grandma, because nobody else ever wrote handwritten letters.

One more letter... I took a deep breath and looked at the return address. It was from Space Camp. It was addressed to me. This was the letter I had been waiting for! I gulped and felt the smooth, stiff envelope. Was the news inside good or bad? Had I won the scholarship?

I really wanted to go to Space Camp. I had spent hours working on the essay that accompanied the application. Mrs. Johnson had sent a great letter of recommendation. But I knew that lots of other fifth graders were anxiously waiting, too. They all probably really wanted to go to Space Camp. They all had probably spent hours on their essays. Their teachers had probably written great letters of recommendation for them. My stomach fluttered, and my mouth went dry.

What news was inside that envelope?

1. Was the character nervous about opening the letter? Tell how you know.
   Yes; gulped, stomach fluttered, mouth was dry

2. What reasons did the character have for being excited about the Space Camp letter?
   He/she spent hours on the essay. His/her teacher wrote a great letter of recommendation.

3. What reasons did the character have for being worried about the contents of the letter?
   Many other students probably spent hours on their essays and had letters of recommendation.

Page 40

Language Bytes

A **common noun** names any person, place, thing, or idea.
A **proper noun** names a specific person, place, thing, or idea.
Proper nouns begin with capital letters.

Write a proper noun for each of the following:

your whole name	Answers will vary but must use capital letters correctly.
your school	
your town	
a song	
a movie	
a mountain	

Math Time

Find the answers.

85 × 35 = **2,975**   51 × 93 = **4,743**   84 × 62 = **5,208**   52 × 10 = **520**

29 × 15 = **435**   124 × 41 = **5,084**   73 × 27 = **1,971**   98 × 40 = **3,920**

73 × 29 = **2,117**   128 × 5 = **640**   219 × 8 = **1,752**   106 × 5 = **530**

Work Space

Work will vary.

Page 41

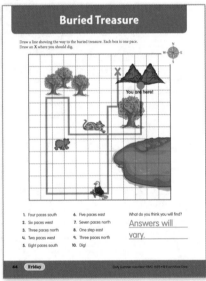

Geography

Antarctica Cross Section

1. What is the approximate elevation of these points?
   Point A — 0 or sea level   Point D — 10 thousand ft.
   Point B — 5 thousand ft.   Point E — –5 thousand ft.
   Point C — –5 thousand ft.   Point F — 5 thousand ft.

2. Do you know the elevation of the place where you live? If not, try to find out.
   Answers will vary.

In My Own Words

You have just received a letter congratulating you on winning a full scholarship to Space Camp. You will learn about spaceflight as you participate in the same kind of training that real astronauts complete. The letter asks you to write a paragraph either accepting or declining the offer. What would you say? Write the paragraph here.

Answers will vary.

Page 42

Language Bytes

Singular nouns name one person, place, thing, or idea. **Plural nouns** name more than one. Complete this paragraph using the plural form of the missing words.

Peter looked around the **cages** There were **kittens** and **puppies** **mice** and **hamsters** There were even some **sheep** The SPCA had **animals** for everyone. He walked up and down the **aisles**, trying to make up his mind. The **animals** watched him with bright **eyes** Some voiced **greetings**, and some moved back into the **corners** of their **cubicles** Peter wished that he could adopt them all.

Math Time

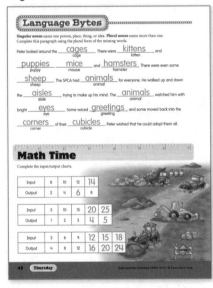

Complete the input/output charts.

Input	8	10	12	14
Output	2	4	6	8

Input	5	10	15	20	25
Output	1	2	3	4	5

Input	3	6	9	12	15	18
Output	4	8	12	16	20	24

Page 43

Language Bytes

Find the groups of words that are sentences. Add end punctuation and write the word **sentence** on the line following each complete sentence. Then add words to each fragment to make it a sentence. Write your new sentences on the lines at the bottom.

Climbed the rock and rested
The leaves rustled in the wind. — **sentence**
The basketball swished through the net. — **sentence**
Pete, Anna, and Paul
Did he go home? — **sentence**

Phrases 1 and 4 should be made into complete sentences.

Math Time

Find the answers.

1. Andy likes to ride his bike. He can ride from his house to school in 10 minutes, from school to Juan's house in 12 minutes, from Juan's house to the mall in 7 minutes, and from the mall to his house in 17 minutes. How long will it take Andy to ride from school to the mall if he rides by Juan's house on the way?
   19 minutes

2. Carla wants to see a movie with her friends to celebrate her birthday. The matinee costs $2.50, and the evening show costs $4.00. If her mother gives her $30.00 to pay for tickets, how many people including Carla can go to the matinee? To the evening show?
   12 people matinee
   7 people evening show

3. Marcos is 48 inches tall. His younger brother, Jose, is 4 inches shorter than Marcos. His older brother, Raul, is 16 inches taller than Jose. How tall is Raul?
   55 inches
   4ft. 7in. feet and inches

Page 44

Buried Treasure

Draw a line showing the way to the buried treasure. Each box is one pace. Draw an **X** where you should dig.

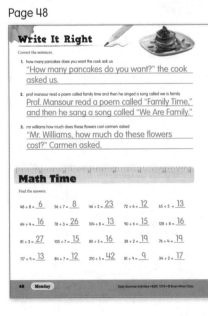

1. Four paces south
2. Six paces west
3. Three paces north
4. Two paces west
5. Eight paces south
6. Five paces east
7. Seven paces north
8. One step east
9. Three paces north
10. Dig!

What do you think you will find?
Answers will vary.

Page 47

Allen Say

Allen Say was born in Yokohama, Japan. When he was six years old, he decided that he wanted to be a cartoonist. However, the world was at war. In the midst of the war, he attended seven different elementary schools. When the war ended, Allen was sent to live with his grandmother. He didn't get along with her, so he was allowed to live alone in a one-room apartment. He was twelve years old when he apprenticed himself to a famous Japanese cartoonist, Noro Shinpei. He spent the next four years drawing and painting.

When Allen was sixteen, his father moved with Allen to the United States. Allen went to a military school in California for one year and then struck out on his own. He moved from job to job, city to city, and school to school. He painted his way through California before he opened a photography studio.

Allen Say has had a long and successful career as a writer, an illustrator, and a photographer. Many of his books tell about parts of his life. His autobiographical story, *Grandfather's Journey*, won the Caldecott Medal in 1994. He has said that it is a joyous experience to tell a story with his brush.

1. What was Allen Say's ambition?
   to be a cartoonist

2. What was unusual about young Allen's life?
   He lived on his own before the age of 12.

3. What does it mean to "apprentice oneself to another person"?
   to work for a master in order to learn a skill

4. What do you do that is a joyous experience?
   Answers will vary.

Check your public library for a book written by Allen Say. *The Apprentice's Trot* is a chapter book that tells about his time as an apprentice.

Page 48

Write It Right

Correct the sentences.

1. how many pancakes does you want the cook ask us
   "How many pancakes do you want?" the cook asked us.

2. prof mansour read a poem called family time and then he singed a song called we is family
   Prof. Mansour read a poem called "Family Time," and then he sang a song called "We Are Family."

3. mr williams how much does these flowers cost carmen asked
   "Mr. Williams, how much do these flowers cost?" Carmen asked.

Math Time

Find the answers.

48 ÷ 8 = **6**   56 ÷ 7 = **8**   46 ÷ 2 = **23**   72 ÷ 6 = **12**   65 ÷ 5 = **13**

64 ÷ 4 = **16**   78 ÷ 3 = **26**   104 ÷ 8 = **13**   90 ÷ 6 = **15**   128 ÷ 8 = **16**

81 ÷ 3 = **27**   105 ÷ 7 = **15**   80 ÷ 5 = **16**   38 ÷ 2 = **19**   76 ÷ 4 = **19**

117 ÷ 9 = **13**   84 ÷ 7 = **12**   210 ÷ 5 = **42**   81 ÷ 9 = **9**   34 ÷ 2 = **17**

Page 49

SPELL IT

Cross out the silent letter or letters in each of the words below. Then use the words to complete the sentences.

knot   daughter   unknown   kneel   brought   written   scissors

1. Kate had to **kneel** down to untie the **knot** in her shoelace.
2. Mrs. Yang's **daughter** used a pair of **scissors** to cut the ribbon on the gift she had **brought** her.
3. This poem was **written** long ago by an **unknown** poet.

Handwriting

Copy these phrases in your best handwriting.

Marvelous, magnificent Monday
Totally terrific Tuesday
Wild and wonderful Wednesday
Thoroughly thrilling Thursday
And finally, fun-filled Friday
What a week!

Marvelous, magnificent Monday.
Totally terrific Tuesday.
Wild and wonderful Wednesday.
Thoroughly thrilling Thursday.
And finally, fun-filled Friday.
What a week!

Page 50

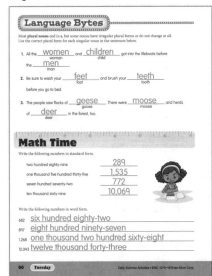

Language Bytes

Most **plural nouns** end in s, but some nouns have irregular plural forms or do not change at all. Use the correct plural form for each singular noun in the sentences below.

1. All the __women__ and __children__ got into the lifeboats before
   woman   child
   the __men__.
          man

2. Be sure to wash your __feet__ and brush your __teeth__
                          foot   tooth
   before you go to bed.

3. The people saw flocks of __geese__. There were __moose__ and herds
                             goose   moose
   of __deer__ in the forest, too.
        deer

Math Time

Write the following numbers in standard form.

two hundred eighty-nine	289
one thousand five hundred thirty-five	1,535
seven hundred seventy-two	772
ten thousand sixty-nine	10,069

Write the following numbers in word form.

682 __six hundred eighty-two__

847 __eight hundred ninety-seven__

1,268 __one thousand two hundred sixty-eight__

12,043 __twelve thousand forty-three__

50   Tuesday   Daily Summer Activities • EMC 1075 • © Evan-Moor Corp.

Page 51

Cut and Paste a Story

When Lois Ehlert went to art school, she discovered that she liked cutting and pasting better than drawing. It was hard to move the parts of a drawing around, but if shapes were cut out of paper they could be moved before they were glued down. So, Ms. Ehlert focused on creating collages. She glued scraps of fabric, ribbon, wire, wrapping paper, plastic, cardboard, seeds, buttons, tree bark, and cardboard flaps. She formed the "found" materials into pictures of the animals, flowers, and trees she loved.

Lois Ehlert's colorful collages illustrate the children's books she has written. When she wrote *Eating the Alphabet*, she spent a year visiting her local grocery store, buying fruits and vegetables, creating bright, bold collages, and eating! Ms. Ehlert has said that every book requires hard work, endless research, and a special idea for presenting the information to her readers.

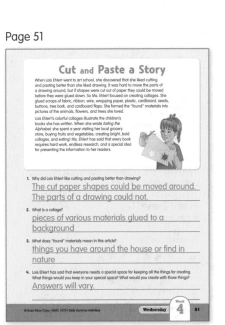

1. Why did Lois Ehlert like cutting and pasting better than drawing?
   __The cut paper shapes could be moved around.__
   __The parts of a drawing could not.__

2. What is a collage?
   __pieces of various materials glued to a__
   __background__

3. What does "found" materials mean in this article?
   __things you have around the house or find in__
   __nature__

4. Lois Ehlert has said that everyone needs a special space for keeping all the things for creating. What things would you keep in your special space? What would you create with those things?
   __Answers will vary.__

© Evan-Moor Corp. • EMC 1075 • Daily Summer Activities   Wednesday Week 4   51

Page 52

Language Bytes

The **tense** of a verb tells when an action occurs.

Underline the verbs in the paragraph below.
Write P over the verb if it happened in the **past**.
Write PR over the verb if it happens in the **present**.
Write F over the verb if it will happen in the **future**.

My cousin promised that she will come for the weekend. She called me last
                         P   F   P
night and said she is coming this evening. She will arrive about 7:00 p.m. Mom is fixing
                    PR   F   F   PR
her favorite dessert as a surprise. We will have a party while she is here.
                                         F   PR

Math Time

Draw the lines of symmetry for each shape.
Then write how many the shape has.

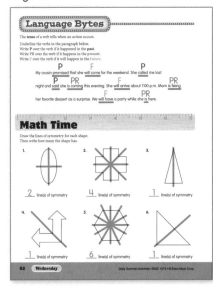

1. __2__ line(s) of symmetry   2. __4__ line(s) of symmetry   3. __1__ line(s) of symmetry

4. __1__ line(s) of symmetry   5. __6__ line(s) of symmetry   6. __1__ line(s) of symmetry

52   Wednesday   Daily Summer Activities • EMC 1075 • © Evan-Moor Corp.

Page 53

Geography

Use a ruler and the map scale to measure the distance between these locations.

Brazil

From	To	Approximate Distance
Rio de Janeiro	Brasília	800 km
São Paulo	Pôrto Alegre	800 km
Pôrto Velho	Brasília	1,600 km

Find two cities on the map that are about 400 km apart.
__Recife and Fortaleza OR__
__São Paulo and Belo Horizonte__

In My Own Words

Make a new word. Use parts of existing words if you'd like.
__Answers will vary.__

What does your word mean? Write its definition.
_____

Use your word in a sentence.
_____

Write about what might happen if you used your new word in a conversation.
_____

© Evan-Moor Corp. • EMC 1075 • Daily Summer Activities   Thursday Week 4   53

Page 54

Language Bytes

We add **ed** to many verbs to make the past tense. Other verbs have spelling changes. These are called **irregular verbs**.

Write the past tense of these verbs.

present	past		present	past
begin	began		choose	chose
grow	grew		eat	ate
run	ran		know	knew
throw	threw		drink	drank
think	thought		write	wrote
make	made		swing	swung

Math Time

Can you put the numbers in order?

1. Rewrite these numbers in order from smallest to largest.

   8.00   8.30   0.800   0.83
   __0.800__ __0.83__ __8.00__ __8.30__
   smallest   largest

   57,327   5,703,275   573,275   5,732
   __5,732__ __57,327__ __573,275__ __5,703,275__
   smallest   largest

2. Write >, <, or = in the circles to make a true statement.

   65.73 ⬤< 65.81   2 ⬤> 1.3   81.0 ⬤= 81.00   3 × 4 ⬤= 6 × 2

54   Thursday   Daily Summer Activities • EMC 1075 • © Evan-Moor Corp.

Page 55

Language Bytes

Pronouns are used as substitutes for nouns.
Circle the pronouns in these sentences. Then write the nouns to which the pronouns refer.

1. The bicycle was ⬤it.   __bicycle__

2. Mario and Lee went to the aquarium because ⬤they wanted   __Mario and Lee__
   to see the new exhibit.   __Elise__

3. Elise said that ⬤she was too busy to do homework last night.

4. Andrea was too big for the old bike, so ⬤she sold ⬤it at a   __Andrea, bike__
   garage sale.   __house__

5. The carpenter built the house and then sold ⬤it.

Math Time

Find the answers.

1. Kiko likes to fish. She caught an 8 pound 3 ounce trout at Ranger Lake. The record catch so far for the season is 124 ounces. Did Kiko's fish break the record? (16 ounces = 1 pound)   __yes__

2. Ian is playing a video game. If he started playing at 3:45 p.m. when he got home from school, and stops playing at 6:15 p.m., how long will Ian have played?   __2 1/2 hours__

3. Henry was getting ready in the morning and noticed that he had four shirts in his closet (red, blue, green, and plaid) as well as three pairs of shorts (denim, white, and black). How many different combinations of one shirt and one pair of shorts can Henry wear?   __12 combinations__

© Evan-Moor Corp. • EMC 1075 • Daily Summer Activities   Friday Week 4   55

Page 56

Building Your Vocabulary

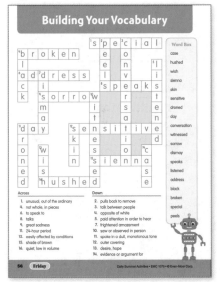

Word Box:
case, hushed, wish, sienna, skin, sensitive, droned, day, conversation, witnessed, sorrow, dismay, speaks, listened, address, black, broken, special, peels

Across
1. unusual, out of the ordinary
4. not whole, in pieces
6. to speak to
8. talks
9. great sadness
11. 24-hour period
13. easily affected by conditions
15. shade of brown
16. quiet, low in volume

Down
2. pulls back to remove
3. talk between people
5. opposite of white
7. paid attention in order to hear
10. frightened amazement
12. saw or observed in person
13. spoke in a dull, monotonous tone
14. outer covering
15. desire, hope
16. evidence or argument for

56   Friday   Daily Summer Activities • EMC 1075 • © Evan-Moor Corp.

Page 59

Loy Krathong

Loy Krathong is a special holiday celebrated in Thailand. *Loy* means "float," and *krathong* means "leaf cup." During the festival, the children of Thailand make little boats from banana leaves. They decorate the sides of their krathongs with colorful flowers and place a candle inside each boat. At nighttime, the children light the candles, make a wish, and watch as their krathongs float down the river. Legend says that if the candle stays lit until the krathong disappears, the wish will come true.

1. Why is Loy Krathong a special holiday?
   __Children light a candle and make a wish.__

2. What would you do to celebrate Loy Krathong? __Put a lighted candle__
   __in a boat made from banana leaves,__
   __make a wish, and let the boat float away.__

3. Write a wish you might make as you put your krathong in the river.
   __Answers will vary.__

4. There are other customs about doing a certain thing to make wishes come true. List several of these customs.
   __blowing out birthday candles__
   __throwing pennies in a wishing well__
   __breaking a wishbone__
   __wishing on a star__

© Evan-Moor Corp. • EMC 1075 • Daily Summer Activities   Monday Week 5   59

Page 60

Write It Right   Thank You.

Correct the sentences.

1. the twins got to write thank-you notes for there birthday presents
   __The twins have to write thank-you notes for__
   __their birthday presents.__

2. how many books did you read this summer asked miss gonzales
   __"How many books did you read this summer?"__
   __asked Miss Gonzales.__

3. i just finished reading harriet the spy anita told henry
   __"I just finished reading Harriet the Spy,"__
   __Anita told Henry.__

Math Time

Find the answers.

584 +392 = 976	467 -232 = 235	738 +295 = 1,033	197 -126 = 71	625 +316 = 941	393 -204 = 189

37 × 9 = __333__   41 × 8 = __328__   96 × 6 = __576__   27 × 7 = __189__   58 × 5 = __290__

41 × 9 = __369__   640 ÷ 8 = __80__   497 ÷ 7 = __71__   828 ÷ 9 = __92__   564 ÷ 6 = __94__

60   Monday   Daily Summer Activities • EMC 1075 • © Evan-Moor Corp.

Page 61

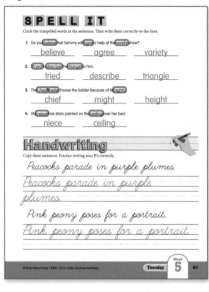

S P E L L I T

Circle the misspelled words in the sentences. Then write them correctly on the lines.

1. Do you ⟨believe⟩ that Sammy will ⟨agre⟩ to help at the ⟨vareity⟩ show?

   believe   agree   variety

2. ⟨Tryed⟩ to ⟨descripe⟩ the ⟨triangel⟩ to him.

   tried   describe   triangle

3. The ⟨cheif⟩ ⟨mite⟩ choose the ladder because of its ⟨hieght⟩.

   chief   might   height

4. My ⟨neece⟩ has stars painted on the ⟨cieling⟩ over her bed.

   niece   ceiling

Handwriting

Copy these sentences. Practice writing your P's correctly.

Peacocks parade in purple plumes.

Peacocks parade in purple plumes.

Pink peony poses for a portrait.

Pink peony poses for a portrait.

Page 62

Language Bytes

Underline the possessive words in these sentences.
Add apostrophes where you need them to show ownership.

1. The sun's rays melted the ice cream.
2. The students' portfolio was stored in the file.
3. The dogs' leashes broke as they chased the cat across the field.
4. The girls' skateboard was left on the playground.

Write a sentence with a possessive that uses 's.

Sentences will vary but should use a singular possessive noun.

Write a sentence with a possessive that uses s'.

Sentences will vary but should use a plural possessive noun.

Math Time

Draw the next figure in each pattern. Then write a sentence describing each pattern.

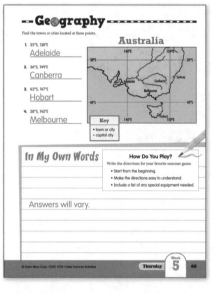

Rule Answers will vary.

Rule

Rule

Page 63

The Science Project

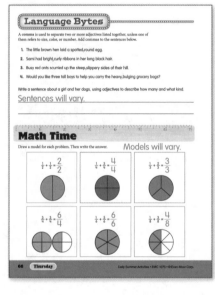

Just before the bell rang, Mr. Nielsen said, "Don't forget that your science projects are due a week from today."

Jose thought about his project. A few days ago, he had found frog eggs at the pond near his house. He had scooped up a dozen or so eggs and some pond water in an empty jar. At home, he placed the jar on top of the refrigerator to stay warm. The eggs looked like small black beads in white jelly.

Each day, Jose looked at the eggs through a magnifying glass and drew what he saw. Day by day, he watched the jelly part of the eggs get smaller as the tadpoles grew in the black centers. Soon he could see heads and tails, and the tadpoles began to move. His science book said that the jelly part was food for the growing tadpoles.

The next Thursday, the first of the eggs hatched. A tiny tadpole stuck itself to a leaf of the pond plant Jose had put in the jar. It had no mouth yet, but Jose could see fingerlike gills behind its head.

By Friday, four more eggs had hatched. Jose carefully carried the jar to school, along with his day-by-day drawings and his journal of the changes he'd seen.

"This is a fine project, Jose," said Mr. Nielsen. "You must have given it a lot of thought."

Number these sentences in the order in which they happened.

3   The tadpoles began to hatch.

5   On Friday, Jose took his science project to school.

6   Mr. Nielsen liked Jose's science project.

1   Jose found frog eggs in the pond and took some home in a jar.

4   The young tadpoles had gills but no mouths.

2   Each day the black part of the eggs grew to look more like tadpoles.

Page 64

Language Bytes

Some possessives do not need apostrophes.
Circle the possessive form in each of these sentences.

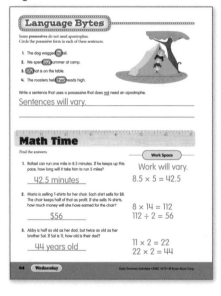

1. The dog wagged ⟨its⟩ tail.
2. We spent ⟨our⟩ summer at camp.
3. ⟨My⟩ hat is on the table.
4. The roosters held ⟨their⟩ heads high.

Write a sentence that uses a possessive that does not need an apostrophe.

Sentences will vary.

Math Time

Find the answers.

Work Space

Work will vary.

1. Rafael can run one mile in 8.5 minutes. If he keeps up this pace, how long will it take him to run 5 miles?

   42.5 minutes $8.5 \times 5 = 42.5$

2. Maria is selling T-shirts for her choir. Each shirt sells for $8. The choir keeps half of that as profit. If she sells 14 shirts, how much money will she have earned for the choir?

   $56 $8 \times 14 = 112$
               $112 \div 2 = 56$

3. Abby is half as old as her dad. If Sal is 11, how old is her dad?

   44 years old $11 \times 2 = 22$
                       $22 \times 2 = 44$

Page 65

Geography

Find the towns or cities located at these points.

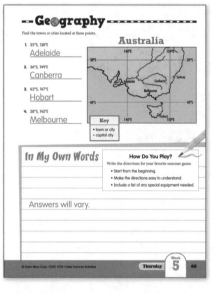

Australia

1. 35°S, 138°E   Adelaide
2. 35°S, 149°E   Canberra
3. 43°S, 147°E   Hobart
4. 38°S, 145°E   Melbourne

Key
• town or city
• capital city

In My Own Words

Write the directions for your favorite summer game.

How Do You Play?
• Start from the beginning.
• Make the directions easy to understand.
• Include a list of any special equipment needed.

Answers will vary.

Page 66

Language Bytes

A comma is used to separate two or more adjectives listed together, unless one of them refers to size, color, or number. Add commas to the sentences below.

1. The little brown hen laid a spotted, round egg.
2. Sami had bright, curly ribbons in her long black hair.
3. Busy red ants scurried up the steep, slippery sides of their hill.
4. Would you like three tall boys to help you carry the heavy, bulging grocery bags?

Write a sentence about a girl and her dogs, using adjectives to describe how many and what kind.

Sentences will vary.

Math Time

Draw a model for each problem. Then write the answer.   Models will vary.

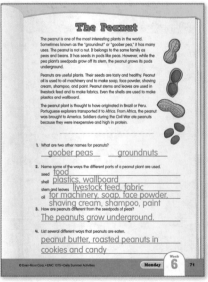

$\frac{1}{2} + \frac{1}{2} = \frac{2}{2}$ $\frac{1}{4} + \frac{3}{4} = \frac{4}{4}$ $\frac{1}{3} + \frac{2}{3} = \frac{3}{3}$

$\frac{3}{4} + \frac{3}{4} = \frac{6}{4}$ $\frac{1}{6} + \frac{5}{6} = \frac{6}{6}$ $\frac{1}{8} + \frac{3}{8} = \frac{4}{8}$

Page 67

Language Bytes

Use **this** with singular nouns. Use **these** with plural nouns.
Complete each sentence using this or these.

1. This   slice of cake is yummy.
2. Will you help me put   these   chairs away?
3. This   is the steepest hill in the neighborhood.
4. I want to put   these   books in my backpack.

Write a sentence using this as an adjective.

Sentences will vary.

Write a sentence using these as an adjective.

Math Time

Draw a model for each problem. Then write the answer.   Models will vary.

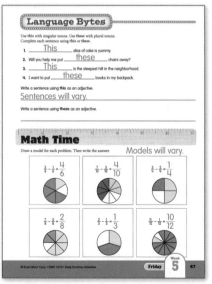

$\frac{5}{6} - \frac{1}{6} = \frac{4}{6}$ $\frac{7}{10} - \frac{3}{10} = \frac{4}{10}$ $\frac{3}{4} - \frac{2}{4} = \frac{1}{4}$

$\frac{7}{8} - \frac{5}{8} = \frac{2}{8}$ $\frac{2}{3} - \frac{1}{3} = \frac{1}{3}$ $\frac{11}{12} - \frac{1}{12} = \frac{10}{12}$

Page 68

Syllogisms

Long ago in Greece, a famous thinker named Aristotle invented the **syllogism**. A syllogism has three parts. Facts are given in the first two parts. The third part is a new idea taken from the facts in the first two parts.

Example: All birds have feathers.
Chickens are birds.
Therefore, chickens have feathers.

A syllogism can be valid without being true.

Example: All babies are cute.
No cute things cry.
Therefore, no babies cry.

Write the third line for each of the following syllogisms.
Mark whether you think the syllogism is true or false.

All children like bubble gum.
All girls are children.
Therefore, all girls like bubble gum   True   ⟨False⟩

All kinds of fruit are sweet.
Lemons are a kind of fruit.
Therefore, lemons are sweet   True   ⟨False⟩

All stars are in the sky.
The sun is a star.
Therefore, the sun is in the sky   ⟨True⟩   False

All apples grow on trees.
Granny Smiths are apples.
Therefore, Granny Smiths grow on trees   ⟨True⟩   False

Page 71

The Peanut

The peanut is one of the most interesting plants in the world. Sometimes known as the "groundnut" or "goober pea," it has many uses. The peanut is not a nut. It belongs to the same family as peas and beans. It has seeds in pods like peas. However, while the pea plant's seedpods grow off its stem, the peanut grows its pods underground.

Peanuts are useful plants. Their seeds are tasty and healthy. Peanut oil is used to oil machinery and to make soap, face powder, shaving cream, shampoo, and paint. Peanut stems and leaves are used in livestock feed and to make fabrics. Even the shells are used to make plastics and wallboard.

The peanut plant is thought to have originated in Brazil or Peru. Portuguese explorers transported it to Africa. From Africa, the peanut was brought to America. Soldiers during the Civil War ate peanuts because they were inexpensive and high in protein.

1. What are two other names for peanuts?

   goober peas   groundnuts

2. Name some of the ways the different parts of a peanut plant are used.

   seed   food
   shell   plastics, wallboard
   stem and leaves   livestock feed, fabric
   oil   for machinery, soap, face powder, shaving cream, shampoo, paint

3. How are peanuts different from the seedpods of peas?

   The peanuts grow underground.

4. List several different ways that peanuts are eaten.

   peanut butter, roasted peanuts in cookies and candy

Page 72

Write It Right

Correct the sentences.

1. to make the pizza crust mr toscano threw the doe into the air
   To make the pizza crust, Mr. Toscano threw the dough into the air.

2. she called shannon her best friend to find out when the picnic will began
   She called Shannon, her best friend, to find out when the picnic will begin.

3. watch out there is broken glass on the floor yelled peter
   "Watch out! There is broken glass on the floor!" yelled Peter.

Math Time

Add the following fractions.

1. $\frac{1}{7} + \frac{5}{7} = \frac{6}{7}$

2. $\frac{3}{7} + \frac{3}{7} = \frac{6}{7}$

3. $\frac{1}{6} + \frac{4}{6} = \frac{5}{6}$

Add the following mixed fractions.

4. $1\frac{1}{5} + 2\frac{2}{5} = 3\frac{3}{5}$

5. $3\frac{1}{4} + 1\frac{2}{4} = 4\frac{3}{4}$

6. $1\frac{4}{9} + 2\frac{3}{9} = 3\frac{7}{9}$

72　Monday

Page 73

SPELL IT

First draw lines to divide each compound word into syllables. Then write the two words that make up each compound word. Finally, write the number of syllables in each one.

outfield	out	field	2
dragonfly	dragon	fly	3
anybody	any	body	4
keyboard	key	board	2
undercover	under	cover	4
snowflake	snow	flake	2
southwest	south	west	2
secondhand	second	hand	3

Handwriting

Copy these lines from the famous poem *Sea Fever*, by John Masefield. Use your best handwriting.

I must go down to the seas again, to the lonely sea and the sky. And all I ask is a tall ship and a star to steer her by.

I must go down to the seas again, to the lonely sea and the sky. And all I ask is a tall ship and a star to steer her by.

Tuesday Week 6　73

Page 74

Language Bytes

Add **er** to compare two nouns. Add **est** to compare three or more nouns.
Add **er** or **est** to each of the adjectives to complete the sentences.

1. Lizzie is the fast**est** runner in the class.
2. Tyrone is tall**er** than Syd.
3. The fire alarm is the loud**est** thing I've ever heard.
4. A bratwurst is fatt**er** than a hot dog.

Write a sentence comparing two things.
Sentences must use "er" suffix.

Write a sentence comparing three or more things.
Sentences must use "est" suffix.

Math Time

How many containers will you need if...?

4 fish fit in a can　　11 fish fit in a box　　18 fish fit in a crate

number of fish	cans	boxes	crates
16	4	2	1
9	3	1	1
25	7	3	2
37	10	4	3
45	12	5	3
75	19	7	5

74　Tuesday

Page 75

George Washington Carver
1860s – 1943

George Washington Carver grew up as an enslaved African American on a plantation in Missouri. As a boy, George loved plants! By the time he was seven or so, people in Diamond Grove, Missouri, called him "The Plant Doctor."

George was a skinny child with a high voice. He talked, but he was determined to learn as much as he could. When he was about ten, he left home to find a town that would allow black children to go to school. He traveled through Missouri and Kansas, going to schools that would accept him, until he graduated from high school. He did laundry to pay his expenses.

In 1890, George began college. He studied art and then agriculture. He was the first black graduate of Iowa State College. Thomas Edison asked George to come to work in his laboratory, but George turned him down. George said that he wanted to help his people. So he set up an agricultural department at Tuskegee Normal School, a new university for black students in Alabama.

George Washington Carver became known as the "Wizard of Tuskegee." His work was instrumental in improving farming in the South. He is especially remembered for his peanut research. He discovered more than 300 uses for the peanut plant.

1. What words would you use to describe George Washington Carver?
   determined, smart, hardworking, etc.

2. What makes Dr. Carver's story so inspirational?
   He began life as a slave and became an important scientist.

3. In this word search, find some of the products that Dr. Carver made from peanuts.

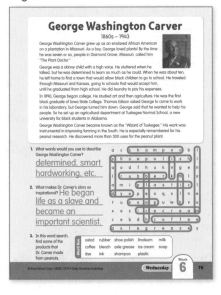

Word Box: salad　rubber　shoe polish　linoleum　milk　coffee　bleach　axle grease　ice cream　soap　dye　ink　shampoo　plastic

© Evan-Moor Corp. • EMC 1075 • Daily Summer Activities　Wednesday Week 6　75

Page 76

Language Bytes

Homophones are words that sound the same but have different meanings. Complete each pair of sentences using a pair of homophones from the boxes.

flower / flour

1. Mallory **heard** the baby crying.
   The **herd** of cattle wandered across the fields.

herd / heard

2. I use whole wheat **flour** when I make bread.
   She wore a yellow **flower** in her hair.

choose / chews

3. Alonzo **chews** the gum and then blows a bubble.
   Maria will **choose** which frosting to put on the cake.

weak / week

4. Use the remaining pair of homophones in a sentence.
   Sentences will vary.

Math Time

Find the answers.

1. In the number 26,195, what digit is in
   the thousands place? 6
   the tens place? 9
   the ten-thousands place? 2
   the hundreds place? 1

2. In the number 935,701, what digit is in
   the ones place? 1
   the ten-thousands place? 3
   the tens place? 0
   the hundreds place? 7

3. In the number 6,871,204, what digit is in
   the hundreds place? 2
   the hundred-thousands place? 8
   the millions place? 6
   the ten-thousands place? 7

4. In the number 1,0674, what digit is in
   the tens place? 6
   the tenths place? 4
   the thousands place? 1
   the ones place? 7

76　Wednesday

Page 77

Geography
Australia

This graph shows the population of the states and territories of Australia. Use the information to write the population of each state or territory and answer the question.

Western Australia　2.6 million
South Australia　1.7 million
Queensland　4.9 million
Northern Territory　.2 million
New South Wales　7.8 million
Victoria　6.2 million
Australian Capital Territory　.4 million
Tasmania　.5 million

How does the population of Victoria compare with the population of South Australia?
Victoria has about 4.5 million more people than South Australia.

In My Own Words

Summer Is Here!
Write a chant or a cheer for summer. Practice reading it aloud. You may even want to make up actions to go with your words.
Example: Sunny day, sunny day,
Bright, bold, squinty ray,
Sunny day, sunny day,
Let's go out and play.

Chants will vary.

Thursday Week 6　77

Page 78

Language Bytes

Use a **preposition** from the word box to complete each sentence.

1. The river ran **under** the bridge.
2. Did you get a letter **from** your grandma?
3. Maria went swimming **with** her friends.
4. I can take messages **for** Dad when he's not home.
5. Don't forget to put a stamp **on** the envelope.
6. Scott ate the largest piece **of** pizza.

Word Box: of　under　for　from　on　with

Write a sentence using two of the words in the word box.
Sentences will vary.

Math Time

Find the answers.

1. Lanie and Fred are each collecting baseball cards. If Lanie has three times as many cards as Fred, and she has 84, how many cards does Fred have?
   28 cards

2. Terry has just set up a 10-gallon fish tank in his bedroom. He has 10 neon tetras, twice as many guppies as tetras, and half as many blue gouramis as tetras. How many fish does he have in all?
   35 fish

3. Matt has 4 pet rats. Eric has 2 parakeets. Kirstin has 3 gerbils. If each pet eats one-quarter cup of food each day, how much food do they need altogether for 8 days?
   18 cups

Work Space
Work will vary.
$84 \div 3 = 28$

10
$10 \times 2 = 20$
$10 \div 2 = 5$

$4 + 2 + 3 = 9$
$9 \times .25 = 2.25$
$2.25 \times 8 = 18$

78　Thursday

Page 79

Language Bytes

Write **contractions** to complete the sentences.

I'm going to the park to play. My friend Thomas **can't** come with me.
(I am) (can not)

His mother **isn't** feeling well, so we will stay home. After **I've** finished playing, **I'll** go to the library and check out a book. Then **I'll** take the book over to Thomas so he **won't** feel lonely.
(is not) (I have) (I will) (I will) (will not)

Math Time

Solve the problems. Then use the key to answer the riddles.

What has eyes but cannot see?　P O T A T O

662	504	734	426	845	615
-275	-166	-157	-379	-268	-277
387	338	577	47	577	338

What has ears but cannot hear?　C O R N

356	723	783	912
-278	-385	-388	-667
78	338	395	245

What has a tongue but cannot talk?　S H O E

614	524	836	347
-187	-297	-498	-168
427	227	338	179

Key: 47 = a　227 = h　395 = r　78 = c　245 = n
179 = e　338 = o　577 = t　387 = p　427 = s

Friday Week 6　79

Page 83

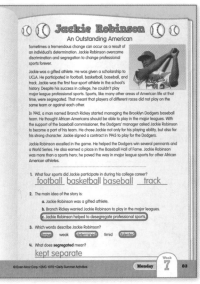

Jackie Robinson
An Outstanding American

Sometimes a tremendous change can occur as a result of an individual's determination. Jackie Robinson overcame discrimination and segregation to change professional sports forever.

Jackie was a gifted athlete. He was given a scholarship to UCLA. He participated in football, basketball, baseball, and track. Jackie was the first four-sport athlete in the school's history. Despite his success in college, he couldn't play major league professional sports. Sports, like many other areas of American life at that time, were segregated. That meant that players of different races did not play on the same team or against each other.

In 1942, a man named Branch Rickey started managing the Brooklyn Dodgers baseball team. He thought African Americans should be able to play in the major leagues. With the support of the baseball commissioner, the Dodgers' manager asked Jackie Robinson to become a part of his team. He chose Jackie not only for his playing ability, but also for his strong character. Jackie signed a contract in 1945 to play for the Dodgers.

Jackie Robinson excelled in the game. He helped the Dodgers win several pennants and a World Series. He also earned a place in the Baseball Hall of Fame. Jackie Robinson was more than a sports hero; he paved the way in major league sports for other African American athletes.

1. What four sports did Jackie participate in during his college career?
   football　basketball　baseball　track

2. The main idea of the story is:
   a. Jackie Robinson was a gifted athlete.
   b. Branch Rickey wanted Jackie Robinson to play in the major leagues.
   c. Jackie Robinson helped to desegregate professional sports.

3. Which words describe Jackie Robinson?
   brave　weak　determined　timid　talented

4. What does **segregated** mean?
   kept separate

Monday Week 7　83

Page 84

Write It Right

Correct the sentences.

1. the clouds rolled in the sky turned dark and it began to snow
   The clouds rolled in, the sky turned dark, and it began to snow.

2. yes maurice I want you to correct the mistakes on this paper said mr yamaguchi
   "Yes, Maurice, I want you to correct the mistakes on this paper," said Mr. Yamaguchi.

3. cody have drew a diagram of the heart lungs and liver of a mouse
   Cody has drawn (or drew) a diagram of the heart, lungs, and liver of a mouse.

Math Time

Find the answers. Show your work.   Work will vary.

1. 960 ÷ 4 = **240**

2. 917 ÷ 7 = **131**

3. 5,498 ÷ 2 = **2,749**

4. 8,580 ÷ 5 = **1,716**

Page 85

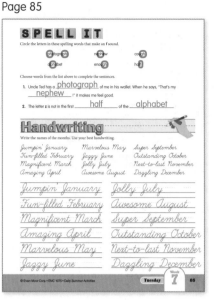

SPELL IT

Circle the letters in these spelling words that make an **f** sound.

photo**ph**, ne**ph**ew, cou**gh**
al**ph**abet, enou**gh**, hal**f**

Choose words from the list above to complete the sentences.

1. Uncle Ted has a **photograph** of me in his wallet. When he says, "That's my **nephew**!" it makes me feel good.

2. The letter z is not in the first **half** of the **alphabet**.

Handwriting

Write the names of the months. Use your best handwriting.

Jumpin' January   Marvelous May   Super September
Fun-filled February   Jazzy June   Outstanding October
Magnificent March   Jolly July   Next-to-last November
Amazing April   Awesome August   Dazzling December

Jumpin' January   Jolly July
Fun-filled February   Awesome August
Magnificent March   Super September
Amazing April   Outstanding October
Marvelous May   Next-to-last November
Jazzy June   Dazzling December

Page 86

Language Bytes

Write the correct **abbreviation** for each word.

qt.   Ave.   lb.   Jr.   St.
tbsp.   cm   Mr.   Dr.   ft.

Avenue	**Ave.**	Street	**St.**
Mister	**Mr.**	tablespoon	**tbsp.**
foot	**ft.**	Junior	**Jr.**
pound	**lb.**	quart	**qt.**
Doctor	**Dr.**	centimeter	**cm**

Math Time

Find the answers.   **Work Space**

1. Maurice is three times as tall as his brother. If Maurice is 5 feet, 3 inches tall, how tall is his brother? (Hint: Change Maurice's height to inches.)
   21 inches tall   Work will vary.
                            63 ÷ 3 = 21

2. Betty has 15 beanbag animals. If she gives ⅓ of them to her sister, how many will she have left?
   10 beanbag animals   15 ÷ 3 = 5
                            15 − 5 = 10

3. Murphy is walking dogs to earn some spending money. If he gets paid $2.50 per dog, and he needs $18.00, how many dogs must he walk?
   8 dogs   18 ÷ 2.5 = 7.2

Page 87

The Antarctic Ozone Hole

Ozone is a gas, a form of oxygen. A layer of ozone in the Earth's atmosphere protects Earth and its living things from dangerous ultraviolet radiation in the sun's rays. In 1985, scientists discovered a hole in the ozone layer over Antarctica. The hole is actually a large area with extremely low levels of ozone gas. The low levels usually appear around September and then return to normal by December. However, scientists concluded that pollution from synthetic chemicals was causing the ozone to become thinner. Synthetic chemicals are used in cleaning products, cooling fluid in refrigerators, and aerosol sprays.

In 2006, scientists discovered that the ozone hole was the largest it had ever been, covering 10 million square miles (26 million square km). Since then, the hole has become slightly smaller, and ozone levels have increased, though they are still far below what they were 30 years ago. Despite this short-term improvement, many scientists still fear that the ozone hole could cause damage to the ice, fish, and marine plants in Antarctica.

1. What is the ozone layer?
   a layer of gas in Earth's atmosphere

2. Why is the ozone layer important?
   It protects Earth from dangerous ultraviolet radiation in the sun's rays.

3. What do scientists think is the cause of the ozone hole?
   synthetic chemicals used in cleaning products, cooling fluid in refrigerators, and aerosol sprays

4. What are the possible effects of a decrease in ozone levels?
   It could cause damage to the ice, fish, and marine plants in Antarctica.

Page 88

Language Bytes

Add **commas** to these sentences.

1. Tanya, welcome to our class!

2. I can tell, Jamal, that you've been practicing.

3. I can help you Monday, Grandma.

4. Okay, Mom. I'm on my way.

5. Say, can you tell me how to do this problem?

6. Hurry up, Mark, or we're going to be late.

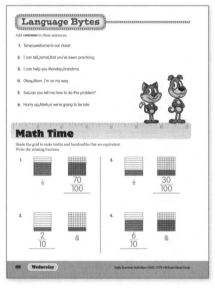

Math Time

Shade the grid to make tenths and hundredths that are equivalent. Write the missing fractions.

1. — = 70/100

2. — = 2/10

3. — = 30/100

4. — = 6/10

Page 89

Geography

Name the countries and the bodies of water marked on this map.

A. **Pacific Ocean**
B. **Gulf of Mexico**
C. **Atlantic Ocean**
D. **Hudson Bay**
E. **Bering Sea**
F. **Canada**
G. **United States**
H. **Mexico**

United States, Canada, Mexico, Atlantic Ocean, Pacific Ocean, Gulf of Mexico, Hudson Bay, Bering Sea

In My Own Words   That's Alliteration!

Write three sentences in which every word begins with the same sound.

Begin by trying one with your own name.   Example: Jill jumped John's juniper joyfully.

1. **Answers will vary.**

2.

3.

Page 90

Language Bytes

Add **commas** to this letter.

410 Park Street
Funville, Ohio 43000
July 30, 2000

Dear Pete,

Thank you for the super new shirt. I like the logo, the color, and the material. You sure know how to pick out a good present! I hope that you can come to visit soon. We can go to the zoo, have a picnic, and see a movie. Thanks again.

Your pal,
Fred

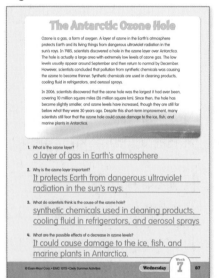

Math Time

Find the answer.

1. What are the common factors of 16 and 24?
   1, 2, 4, 8

2. What are the first three common multiples of 6 and 8?
   24, 48, 72

3. Match each number to its set of multiples.
   6 — 16, 24, 32, 40, 48
   5 — 10, 15, 20, 25, 30
   8 — 12, 18, 24, 30, 36

4. Give all the factors of 8.
   1, 2, 4, 8

Page 91

Language Bytes

Add **quotation marks** to these sentences.

1. "How long will the movie last?" wondered Tamara.

2. "Fernando, will you get the bat?" asked Coach Danley.

3. On the way home from the pool, Simon said, "I can't wait to warm up!"

4. "I can't eat spinach," said Fred. "I might turn green!"

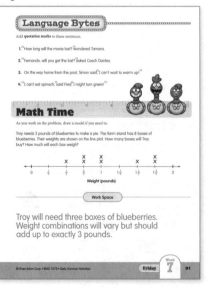

Math Time

As you work on the problem, draw a model if you need to.

Troy needs 3 pounds of blueberries to make a pie. The farm stand has 8 boxes of blueberries. Their weights are shown on the line plot. How many boxes will Troy buy? How much will each box weigh?

(line plot: Weight (pounds), 0 to 2)

Work Space

Troy will need three boxes of blueberries. Weight combinations will vary but should add up to exactly 3 pounds.

Page 92

Number Puzzle

1. Choose three different digits from 1 to 9.   **3, 2, 1**

2. Make the largest and the smallest numbers you can from the three digits.
   321
   − 123

3. Subtract the smaller number from the larger number.
   198

4. Reverse the order of the digits in the answer, and add it to the original answer.
   + 891
   1,089

5. Write the answer.

Try it with three digits other than 3, 2, 1.	Try it with four different digits.
1,089	10,890

How did the answer change from 3 digits to 4 digits?
The answer was multiplied by 10.

Do you think the same thing will happen if you try it with 5 digits?   Yes   No   **Answers will vary.**
Try it and see.

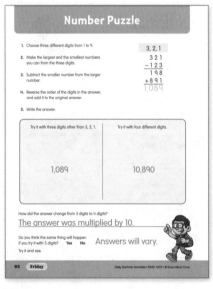

Page 95

Please fill out this application in your best handwriting.

Whatever You Dream Camp

Gymnastics
Baseball **Soccer**
Space Cooking Science
Music Horseback Riding

APPLICATION
Answers will vary.

First Name | Middle Initial | Last Name | Area Code | Telephone
Street Address | City | State | Zip Code
School | Grade | Age | Date of Birth
Full Name of Parent or Guardian | Best Way to Contact Parent or Guardian

If you could go to any kind of camp you wanted, what kind would you choose?

Why would you like to go to this kind of camp?

Page 96

Write It Right

Correct the sentences.

1. him and me got a reward for finding jeannies lost dog
   He and I got a reward for finding Jeannie's lost dog.

2. sean had ate popcorn nachos and too hot dogs at the ball game
   Sean ate popcorn, nachos, and two hot dogs at the ball game.

3. your parents are celebrating there fifteenth anniversary in august
   Your parents are celebrating their fifteenth anniversary in August.

Math Time

Find the answers.

Work Space

Work will vary.

1. The sleepover party ended at 11:45 a.m. If the party lasted 16 hours and 30 minutes, at what time did the party start?
   7:15 p.m.

2. Sven can buy a candy bar from the grocery store for 30 cents, but the gas station sells them three for $1.00. Which is the better buy?
   grocery store

3. Diego was traveling about 30 miles per hour while racing his dirt bike. If he kept up this speed for one and one-half hours, about how many miles would he have traveled?
   45 miles

Page 97

SPELL IT

Fill in the missing letters to write the spelling words.

oi   oy
v_oi_ce   _oi_al
v_oy_age   disapp_oi_nt
n_oi_se   destr_oy

u   ew   ue
tr_u_th   n_ew_s
d_ue   _u_sed
_u_niform   f_u_ture

Handwriting

Write these ice-cream flavors.

rocky road and vanilla
strawberry and bubble gum
butter pecan and chocolate
cookies 'n cream and lemon sour

rocky road and vanilla
strawberry and bubble gum
butter pecan and chocolate
cookies 'n cream and lemon sour

What's your favorite flavor? Why?
Answers will vary.

Page 98

Write It Right

Correct the sentences. Use capital letters where they are needed.

1. jo said that jungle book was her favorite movie
   Jo said that Jungle Book was her favorite movie.

2. my friend joyce lives in evanston illinois
   My friend Joyce lives in Evanston, Illinois.

3. dr cook said that i could get my cast off on august 4
   Dr. Cook said that I could get my cast off on August 4.

Math Time

Find the answers.

51 × 65 = 3,315   67 × 54 = 3,618   38 × 72 = 2,736   24 × 93 = 2,232

74 × 86 = 6,364   93 × 24 = 2,232   48 × 75 = 3,600   13 × 83 = 1,079

Page 99

Colorful Ramblings
from a Crayon Box

"Boy, is it crowded in here! That Jungle Green is in my spot! Will you please move? I wish they would make these boxes bigger!"

"Stop complaining! Soon one of us will be lost or broken, and then there'll be plenty of room."

I listened and observed as the hushed conversation in my crayon box droned on. It was a new 64-color box with a tight lid and bright yellow and green triangles covering its front.

Few crayon users realize that crayons not only speak, but they also have feelings. Just the other day, I witnessed the dismay of a Canary Yellow whose tip was nibbled off by a hungry artist. Have you ever seen the sorrow of a 20-color box that lost its black? Imagine life without a black crayon! You see, crayons have the sensitive souls of artists.

The next time you use a crayon, think about the fragile feelings hidden under the ripped paper covering. Think of the shame and hopelessness in the lost-crayon tub. Take the time to return your crayons to their rightful home. Use them wisely so that their creative potential is realized.

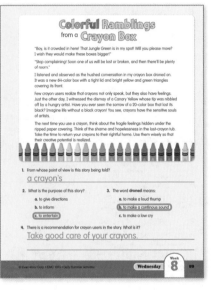

1. From whose point of view is this story being told?
   a crayon's

2. What is the purpose of this story?
   a. to give directions
   b. to inform
   c. to entertain

3. The word droned means:
   a. to make a loud thump
   b. to make a continuous sound
   c. to make a low cry

4. There is a recommendation for crayon users in the story. What is it?
   Take good care of your crayons.

Page 100

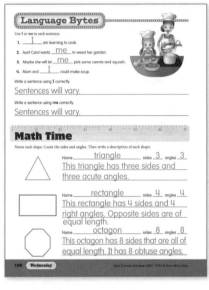

Language Bytes

Use I or me in each sentence.

1. _I_ am learning to cook.
2. Aunt Carol wants _me_ to weed her garden.
3. Maybe she will let _me_ pick some carrots and squash.
4. Mom and _I_ could make soup.

Write a sentence using I correctly.
Sentences will vary.

Write a sentence using me correctly.
Sentences will vary.

Math Time

Name each shape. Count the sides and angles. Then write a description of each shape.

Name __triangle__ sides _3_ angles _3_
This triangle has three sides and three acute angles.

Name __rectangle__ sides _4_ angles _4_
This rectangle has 4 sides and 4 right angles. Opposite sides are of equal length.

Name __octagon__ sides _8_ angles _8_
This octagon has 8 sides that are all of equal length. It has 8 obtuse angles.

Page 101

Geography

Locate each body of water on this map. Write its letter.

C Caribbean Sea
E Gulf of California
F Arctic Ocean
B Great Lakes
D Rio Grande
A Mississippi River

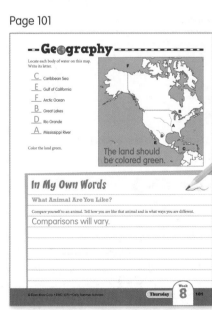

The land should be colored green.

Color the land green.

In My Own Words

What Animal Are You Like?

Compare yourself to an animal. Tell how you are like that animal and in what ways you are different.
Comparisons will vary.

Page 102

Language Bytes

Complete each sentence using the correct word from the box. Then circle the words.

1. How _well_ did you do?
2. _Our_ kittens are growing bigger.
3. _Who's_ that boy standing by the pool?
4. Cookies fresh out of the oven taste so _good_.
5. Do you know _whose_ hat this is?
6. When _are_ you going on vacation?

good   well
Are   our
who's   Whose
good   well
who's   whose
are   our

Math Time

Subtract the following fractions.

1. $\frac{7}{9} - \frac{3}{9} = \frac{4}{9}$
2. $\frac{6}{7} - \frac{1}{7} = \frac{5}{7}$
3. $\frac{3}{4} - \frac{2}{4} = \frac{1}{4}$
4. $\frac{8}{9} - \frac{1}{9} = \frac{7}{9}$
5. $\frac{4}{5} - \frac{2}{5} = \frac{2}{5}$

Subtract the following mixed fractions.

6. $6\frac{3}{4} - 1\frac{1}{4} = 5\frac{2}{4}$ OR $5\frac{1}{2}$
7. $5\frac{5}{6} - 1\frac{3}{6} = 4\frac{2}{6}$
8. $6\frac{6}{7} - 2\frac{1}{7} = 4\frac{5}{7}$
9. $5\frac{5}{8} - 2\frac{2}{8} = 3\frac{3}{8}$
10. $8\frac{7}{8} - 5\frac{6}{8} = 3\frac{1}{8}$

Page 103

Language Bytes

Circle all the nouns in this list.

bake Trina school hospital long truck from pickle
Mr. Gorze contest Mr. Gorze watermelon funny Disneyland park happy

Write the nouns you circled in the correct category.

Person	Place	Thing
Trina	school	truck
Mr. Gorze	hospital	feather
friend	Disneyland	watermelon
Tom	park	pickle

Math Time

Maria is setting up a lemonade stand. She will sell a glass of lemonade for 20 cents and a cookie for $1.20. Help her complete the chart she will use.

	Price of Lemonade	Price of Cookies	Price of Lemonade + Cookies
1	20¢	$1.20	$1.40
2	40¢	$2.40	$2.80
3	60¢	$3.60	$4.20
4	80¢	$4.80	$5.60
5	$1.00	$6.00	$7.00
6	$1.20	$7.20	$8.40

Page 104

Mind Jigglers

Hink Pinks

Hink Pinks are rhyming words that are the answers to clues. For example, an obese feline is a fat cat. See if you can identify these other hink pinks.

1. an unhappy father: **sad dad**
2. a funny young female horse: **silly filly**
3. an uncovered seat: **bare chair**
4. a contest with fire: **flame game**
5. a hog dance: **pig jig**
6. a loyal color: **true blue**
7. not a real cobra: **fake snake**
8. a frog relative on the highway: **road toad**
9. a library burglar: **book crook**
10. 24 hours of games: **play day**
11. a twisted penny: **bent cent**
12. an intelligent body organ: **smart heart**
13. an orca prison: **whale jail**
14. a hilarious rabbit: **funny bunny**
15. 50 percent of a giggle: **half laugh**
16. an ill young chicken: **sick chick**

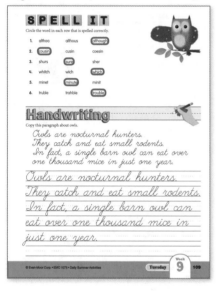

104 — Friday — Daily Summer Activities • EMC 1075 • © Evan-Moor Corp.

Page 107

On Becoming a Climber

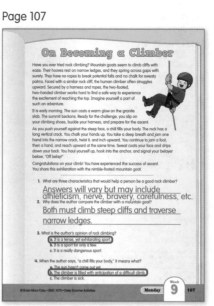

Have you ever tried rock climbing? Mountain goats seem to climb cliffs with ease. Their hooves rest on narrow ledges, and they spring across gaps with surety. They have no ropes to break potential falls and no chalk for sweaty palms. Faced with a similar rock cliff, the human climber often struggles upward. Secured by a harness and ropes, the two-footed, two-handed climber works hard to find a safe way to experience the excitement of reaching the top. Imagine yourself a part of such an adventure.

It is early morning. The sun casts a warm glow on the granite slab. The summit beckons. Ready for the challenge, you slip on your climbing shoes, buckle your harness, and prepare for the ascent.

As you push yourself against the steep face, a chill fills your body. The rock has a long vertical crack. You chalk your hands up. You take a deep breath and jam one hand into the narrow crack, twist it, and inch upward. You continue to jam a foot, then a hand, and reach upward at the same time. Sweat coats your face and drips down your back. You haul yourself up, hook into the anchor, and signal your belayer below. "Off belay!"

Congratulations on your climb! You have experienced the success of ascent. You share this exhilaration with the nimble-footed mountain goat.

1. What are three characteristics that would help a person be a good rock climber?
   Answers will vary but may include athleticism, nerve, bravery, carefulness, etc.

2. Why does the author compare the climber to a mountain goat?
   Both must climb steep cliffs and traverse narrow ledges.

3. What is the author's opinion of rock climbing?
   a. **It is a tense, yet exhilarating sport.**
   b. It is a sport for only a few.
   c. It is a really dangerous sport.

4. When the author says, "a chill fills your body," it means what?
   a. The sun hasn't come out yet.
   b. **The climber is filled with anticipation of a difficult climb.**
   c. The climber is sick.

© Evan-Moor Corp. • EMC 1075 • Daily Summer Activities — Monday — Week 9 — 107

Page 108

Write It Right

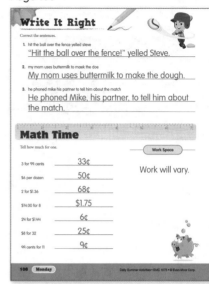

Correct the sentences.

1. hit the ball over the fence yelled steve
   "Hit the ball over the fence!" yelled Steve.

2. my mom uses buttermilk to maek the doe
   My mom uses buttermilk to make the dough.

3. he phoned mike his partner to tell him about the match
   He phoned Mike, his partner, to tell him about the match.

Math Time

Tell how much for one.

3 for 99 cents	**33¢**	Work Space
$6 per dozen	**50¢**	Work will vary.
2 for $1.36	**68¢**	
$14.00 for 8	**$1.75**	
24 for $1.44	**6¢**	
$8 for 32	**25¢**	
99 cents for 11	**9¢**	

108 — Monday — Daily Summer Activities • EMC 1075 • © Evan-Moor Corp.

Page 109

SPELL IT

Circle the word in each row that is spelled correctly.

1. althoa — althous — **although**
2. **cousin** — cusin — coesin
3. shurs — **sure** — sher
4. whitch — wich — **which**
5. minet — **minute** — minit
6. truble — trahble — **trouble**

Handwriting

Copy this paragraph about owls.

Owls are nocturnal hunters. They catch and eat small rodents. In fact, a single barn owl can eat over one thousand mice in just one year.

Owls are nocturnal hunters. They catch and eat small rodents. In fact, a single barn owl can eat over one thousand mice in just one year.

© Evan-Moor Corp. • EMC 1075 • Daily Summer Activities — Tuesday — Week 9 — 109

Page 110

Language Bytes

Add the missing punctuation marks.

comma **,** — colon **:** — period **.**

1. Boston**,**Massachusetts
2. March 7**,**1980
3. 4**:**04 pm**.**
4. Dallas**,**Texas
5. $23**.**95
6. July 4**,**1776

Write today's date. **Answers will vary.**

Write the time. _____

Write the name of your city or town and state. _____

Math Time

Find the answers.

1. Hallie is putting bowls in the cupboard. She can put a maximum of 4 bowls in each stack. If she has 18 bowls to put away, what is the minimum number of stacks Hallie will have?
   5 stacks

   Work Space
   Work will vary.
   $18 \div 4 = 4R2$

2. Mario is going to an amusement park. The park charges 50 cents per ride. Mario wants to ride all 19 rides at least once. What is the minimum amount of money he will need?
   $9.50

   $19 \times .50 = 9.50$

3. Isaiah has a piece of ribbon that is 2 feet long. He wants to cut it into pieces. If each piece is $\frac{1}{2}$ inch long, how many pieces of ribbon will he have?
   48 pieces

   $24 \div .50 = 48$

110 — Tuesday — Daily Summer Activities • EMC 1075 • © Evan-Moor Corp.

Page 111

How Stories Began...

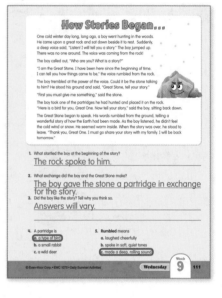

One cold winter day long, long ago, a boy went hunting in the woods. He came upon a great rock and sat down beside it to rest. Suddenly, a deep voice said, "Listen! I will tell you a story." The boy jumped up. There was no one around. The voice was coming from the rock!

The boy called out, "Who are you? What is a story?"

"I am the Great Stone. I have been here since the beginning of time. I can tell you how things came to be," the voice rumbled from the rock.

The boy trembled at the power of the voice. Could it be the stone talking to him? He stood his ground and said, "Great Stone, tell your story."

"First you must give me something," said the stone.

The boy took one of the partridges he had hunted and placed it on the rock. "Here is a bird for you, Great One. Now tell your story," said the boy, sitting back down.

The Great Stone began to speak. His words rumbled from the ground, telling a wonderful story of how the Earth had been made. As the boy listened, he didn't feel the cold wind or snow. He seemed warm inside. When the story was over, he stood to leave. "Thank you, Great One. I must go share your story with my family. I will be back tomorrow."

1. What startled the boy at the beginning of the story?
   The rock spoke to him.

2. What exchange did the boy and the Great Stone make?
   The boy gave the stone a partridge in exchange for the story.

3. Did the boy like the story? Tell why you think so.
   Answers will vary.

4. A partridge is
   a. **a type of bird**
   b. a small rabbit
   c. a wild deer

5. Rumbled means
   a. laughed cheerfully
   b. spoke in soft, quiet tones
   c. **made a deep, rolling sound**

© Evan-Moor Corp. • EMC 1075 • Daily Summer Activities — Wednesday — Week 9 — 111

Page 112

Language Bytes

Use we or us in each sentence.

1. Can **we** make some cookies?
2. It is time for **us** to go to practice.
3. It was fun for **us** to sleep in the tent.
4. **We** have a new kitten.

Write a sentence using **we**.
Sentences will vary.

Write a sentence using **us**.
Sentences will vary.

Math Time

Write >, <, or = in the ○.

$0.143 > 0.34$ $0.51 < 0.60$ $0.88 < 0.89$

$0.30 = 0.3$ $0.20 > 0.02$ $0.10 > 0.01$

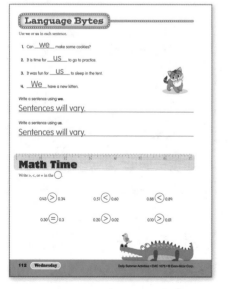

112 — Wednesday — Daily Summer Activities • EMC 1075 • © Evan-Moor Corp.

Page 113

Geography

Using this map, give specific directions for traveling from the Oxley Nature Center to the Philbrook Museum of Art.

Answers will vary.

Tulsa

In My Own Words — Impossible!

Write about something people thought was impossible in the past.
Answers will vary.

Write about something you did that you thought was impossible.

Write about something you think is impossible now but might be possible in the future.

© Evan-Moor Corp. • EMC 1075 • Daily Summer Activities — Thursday — Week 9 — 113

Page 114

Language Bytes

Use can or may in each sentence.

1. **May** I please go to Tori's party?
2. Chelsea runs so fast, she **can** always score a goal.
3. Yvette **can** make a birdhouse without any help.
4. You **can** carry all the groceries inside.
5. You **may** not bring your radio to the dinner table.

Write a sentence using **can**.
Sentences should indicate ability to do something.

Write a sentence using **may**.
Sentences should indicate permission to do something.

Math Time

Choose the correct answer.

1. A baby weighed 8 lb., 3 oz. at birth. At age 3 months, the baby weighed 12 lb., 5 oz. How much weight did the baby gain in three months?
   a. **4 lb. 2 oz**
   b. 5 lb.
   c. 4 lb, 8 oz.

2. The wheelbarrow weighed 30 kilograms when it was full of sand. When empty it weighed 12 kilograms, 25 grams. How much sand does it hold?
   a. 18 kilograms
   b. 17 kilograms, 75 grams
   c. **17 kilograms, 975 grams**

3. The recipe calls for 3 cups of juice to make enough punch for 6 people. How much juice is needed to make punch for one dozen people?
   a. 5 cups
   b. **1 quart, 2 cups**
   c. 1 quart, 3 cups

114 — Thursday — Daily Summer Activities • EMC 1075 • © Evan-Moor Corp.

Page 115

Language Bytes

Complete each sentence using the correct word. Then circle the word.

1. They **play** the game carefully.
2. Mystery stories **are** exciting.
3. My hen **lays** eggs in the nest.
4. The girls **dance** beautifully.

play / **plays**
is / **are**
lay / lays
dance / dances

Write a sentence about a **helicopter**.
Sentences will vary.

Write a sentence about **four snails**.

Math Time

Find the answers.

1. How many feet are in three yards?
   9 feet
2. How many centimeters are in two meters?
   200 centimeters
3. How many inches are in one yard?
   36 inches
4. How many meters are in two and a half kilometers?
   2,500 meters

© Evan-Moor Corp. • EMC 1075 • Daily Summer Activities — Friday Week 9 — 115

Page 116

Analogies

In an analogy, each pair of items has the same relationship.

Bird is to **sky** as **fish** is to **sea**.

Here is a shorter way to write an analogy.

bird : sky :: fish : sea

Choose the correct word to complete the analogy.

1. **Wall** is to **brick** as **skeleton** is to **bone**
   foot, legs, bone, skin
2. **Sail** is to **boat** as **engine** is to **truck**
   truck, battery, drive, bicycle
3. **Hand** is to **mitten** as **head** is to **hat**
   arm, coat, hat, hair
4. **tall** : **short** :: **night** : **day**
   twilight, dark, long, day
5. **flashlight** : **light** :: **furnace** : **heat**
   ice, winter, night, heat
6. **camel** : **desert** :: **ship** : **ocean**
   sand, vehicle, ocean, passenger
7. **closet** : **clothes** :: **refrigerator** : **food**
   house, food, ice cream, kitchen

Analogies...

Write two analogies of your own.
Analogies will vary but must show correct relationship.

116 Friday — Daily Summer Activities • EMC 1075 • © Evan-Moor Corp.

Page 119

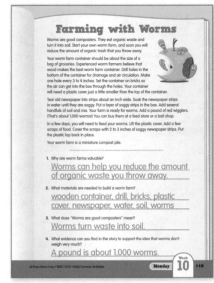

Farming with Worms

Worms are good composters. They eat organic waste and turn it into soil. Start your own worm farm, and soon you will reduce the amount of organic trash that you throw away.

Your worm farm container should be about the size of a bag of groceries. Experienced worm farmers believe that wood makes the best worm farm container. Drill holes in the bottom of the container for drainage and air circulation. Make one hole every 3 to 4 inches. Set the container on bricks so the air can get into the box through the holes. Your container will need a plastic cover just a little smaller than the top of the container.

Tear old newspaper into strips about an inch wide. Soak the newspaper strips in water until they are soggy. Put a layer of soggy strips in the box. Add several handfuls of soil and mix. Your farm is ready for worms. Add a pound of red wigglers. (That's about 1,000 worms.) You can buy them at a feed store or a bait shop.

In a few days, you will need to feed your worms. Lift the plastic cover. Add a few scraps of food. Cover the scraps with 2 to 3 inches of soggy newspaper strips. Put the plastic back in place.

Your worm farm is a miniature compost pile.

1. Why are worm farms valuable?
   Worms can help you reduce the amount of organic waste you throw away.
2. What materials are needed to build a worm farm?
   wooden container, drill, bricks, plastic cover, newspaper, water, soil, worms
3. What does "Worms are good composters" mean?
   Worms turn waste into soil.
4. What evidence can you find in the story to support the idea that worms don't weigh much much?
   A pound is about 1,000 worms.

© Evan-Moor Corp. • EMC 1075 • Daily Summer Activities — Monday Week 10 — 119

Page 120

Write It Right

Correct the sentences.

1. did you see the rattlesnake special on pbs i seen it twice
   Did you see the rattlesnake special on PBS? I saw it twice.
2. me and my family is visiting orlando florida for an week said dr luiz
   "My family and I are visiting Orlando, Florida, for a week," said Dr. Luiz.
3. the coach selected marco my oldest brother two be her helper
   The coach selected Marco, my oldest brother, to be her helper.

Math Time

Find the answer. Explain how you figured it out.

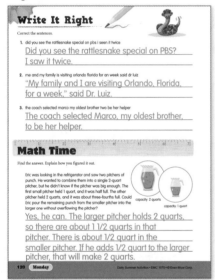

Eric was looking in the refrigerator and saw two pitchers of punch. He wanted to combine them into a single 2-quart pitcher, but he didn't know if the pitcher was big enough. The first small pitcher held 1 quart, and it was half full. The other pitcher held 2 quarts, and it was about three-fourths full. Could Eric pour the remaining punch from the smaller pitcher into the larger one without overflowing the pitcher?

capacity: 2 quarts   capacity: 1 quart

Yes, he can. The larger pitcher holds 2 quarts, so there are about 1 1/2 quarts in that pitcher. There is about 1/2 quart in the smaller pitcher. If he adds 1/2 quart to the larger pitcher, that will make 2 quarts.

120 Monday — Daily Summer Activities • EMC 1075 • © Evan-Moor Corp.

Page 121

S P E L L   I T

What suffixes could you use?

ful   ly   est   less

1. use   ful   less
2. quick   ly   est
3. busy   ly   est
4. large   ly   est
5. worth   less
6. cheer   ful   less
7. harm   ful   less
8. smart   ly   est
9. kind   ly   est

Handwriting

Copy this paragraph in your best handwriting.

Hot sun warms the Earth and causes water to evaporate. When the water vapor rises up into the sky, it meets cold air and condenses into droplets. Millions of drops join to make clouds. When a cloud is full, raindrops fall back to Earth.

Hot sun warms the Earth and causes water to evaporate. When the water vapor rises up into the sky, it meets cold air and condenses into droplets. Millions of drops join to make clouds. When a cloud is full, raindrops fall back to Earth.

© Evan-Moor Corp. • EMC 1075 • Daily Summer Activities — Tuesday Week 10 — 121

Page 122

Language Bytes

Add **es** to each verb. You may have to change **y** to **i** first.

rush **es**   fry **ies**   mix **es**   buzz **es**

Write the correct verb to complete each sentence.

1. Mr. Evans **rushes** to catch the bus.
2. Mom **fries** the bacon for my sandwich.
3. The bee **buzzes** around the jam jar.

Math Time

Write the correct letter or letters to describe each pair of lines.

a = parallel   b = perpendicular   c = intersecting

a //   c X   b, c +

c X   b, c +   a ||

122 Tuesday — Daily Summer Activities • EMC 1075 • © Evan-Moor Corp.

Page 123

The Farming Business

In many parts of the world, farming is a very big business. Farmers need to know much more than how to plant a crop. They need to know how to plan ahead, how machines work, what soil conditions make plants grow well, and how to keep track of money.

To plan their farming year, farmers must know what crops people will buy. They study government reports and other materials to decide what to grow each year.

Some crops require specific kinds of machines to plant, cultivate, or harvest them. The farmer must decide which machines to buy or rent each year. The machinery is purchased or rented with the money from last year's crops.

Some crops require special kinds of soil to grow well. The farmer must study the chemistry of the soil and plan how to make the soil best for the crops. Sometimes fertilizer or chemicals must be purchased to improve the soil.

All this planning requires money. The farmer must keep close track of the money earned by selling the crops. Each year money must be spent on machinery, soil conditioners, and, of course, seed. The farmer must be a good money manager to have a successful farm.

A farmer must combine knowledge of many different occupations to be successful. Explain how a farmer is like:

- a scientist **must study the chemistry of the soil and make the soil best for the crops**
- a mechanic **must know which machines to use and how they work**
- a fortune-teller **must know which crops people will buy**
- a weather forecaster **must know when to plant and when to harvest**
- an accountant **must keep track of money earned and plan for the next year's expenses**

© Evan-Moor Corp. • EMC 1075 • Daily Summer Activities — Wednesday Week 10 — 123

Page 124

Language Bytes

An **adverb** tells how, when, or where.

Circle the adverb that tells about each underlined verb. Then write how, when, or where to tell how the adverb is used.

1. Annie sang quietly to her little sister.   how
2. Carlos practiced ball yesterday.   when
3. When I dropped the box, the cereal flew everywhere.   where
4. The boy waited patiently for his turn.   how

Math Time

Write the answers.

1. Label each angle: **right**, **obtuse**, **acute**.

   A. acute   B. right   C. obtuse

2. Choose the best estimate for each angle.
   A. 30° 60° 70° 100°   30°
   B. 20° 45° 90° 140°   90°
   C. 60° 95° 120° 180°   120°
3. How could you check your estimates? measure with a protractor

124 Wednesday — Daily Summer Activities • EMC 1075 • © Evan-Moor Corp.

Page 125

Geography

1. How many countries are labeled on this map?   5
2. Which country is the largest?   China
3. Which East Asian capital ★ is the farthest...
   east? Tokyo
   west? Ulan Bator
   south? Tokyo
   north? Ulan Bator

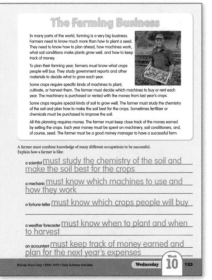

Map labels: Ulan Bator, Mongolia, Beijing, China, North Korea, South Korea, Japan, Tokyo

Key
★ capital

In My Own Words

Make a list of three questions that you would answer "Yes" to.
Questions will vary.

Make a list of three questions that you would answer "No" to.

© Evan-Moor Corp. • EMC 1075 • Daily Summer Activities — Thursday Week 10 — 125

Page 126

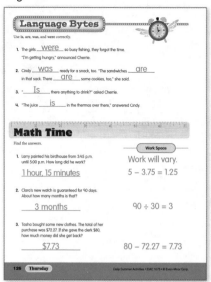

Page 127

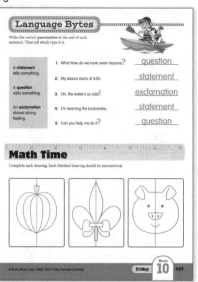

Page 128

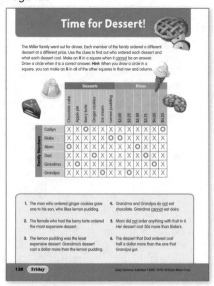

Page 126

Language Bytes

Use **is, are, was,** and **were** correctly.

1. The girls _____were_____ so busy fishing, they forgot the time.
"I'm getting hungry," announced Cherrie.

2. Cindy _____was_____ ready for a snack, too. "The sandwiches _____are_____ in that sack. There _____are_____ some cookies, too," she said.

3. "_____Is_____ there anything to drink?" asked Cherrie.

4. "The juice _____is_____ in the thermos over there," answered Cindy.

Math Time

Find the answers.

Work Space
Work will vary.

1. Larry painted his birdhouse from 3:45 p.m. until 5:00 p.m. How long did he work?

_____1 hour, 15 minutes_____

$5 - 3.75 = 1.25$

2. Clara's new watch is guaranteed for 90 days. About how many months is that?

_____3 months_____

$90 \div 30 = 3$

3. Tasha bought some new clothes. The total of her purchase was $72.27. If she gave the clerk $80, how much money did she get back?

_____$7.73_____

$80 - 72.27 = 7.73$

126 Thursday

Page 127

Language Bytes

Write the correct **punctuation** at the end of each sentence. Then tell which type it is.

A **statement** tells something.

A **question** asks something.

An **exclamation** shows strong feeling.

1. What time do we have swim lessons?   _____question_____

2. My lesson starts at 3:30.   _____statement_____

3. Oh, the water's so cold!   _____exclamation_____

4. I'm learning the backstroke.   _____statement_____

5. Can you help me do it?   _____question_____

Math Time

Complete each drawing. Each finished drawing should be symmetrical.

Friday Week 10 127

Page 128

Time for Dessert!

The Miller family went out for dinner. Each member of the family ordered a different dessert at a different price. Use the clues to find out who ordered each dessert and what each dessert cost. Make an **X** in a square when it cannot be an answer. Draw a circle when it is a correct answer. **Hint:** When you draw a circle in a square, you can make an **X** in all of the other squares in that row and column.

	Chocolate cake	Apple pie	Berry torte	Ginger cookies	Ice cream	Lemon pudding	$3.00	$3.25	$3.50	$3.75	$4.00	$4.25
Caitlyn	X	X	O	X	X	X	X	X	X	X	X	O
Blake	X	X	X	X	O	O	X	X	X	X	X	X
Mom	O	X	X	X	X	X	X	O	X	X	X	X
Dad	X	X	X	O	X	X	X	X	O	X	X	X
Grandma	X	O	X	X	X	X	X	X	X	O	X	X
Grandpa	X	X	X	X	O	X	O	X	X	X	X	X

1. The man who ordered ginger cookies gave one to his son, who likes lemon pudding.

2. The female who had the berry torte ordered the most expensive dessert.

3. The lemon pudding was the least expensive dessert. Grandma's dessert cost a dollar more than the lemon pudding.

4. Grandma and Grandpa do not eat chocolate. Grandma cannot eat dairy.

5. Mom did not order anything with fruit in it. Her dessert cost 50¢ more than Blake's.

6. The dessert that Dad ordered cost half a dollar more than the one that Grandpa got.

128 Friday

Multiplication Table

×	1	2	3	4	5	6	7	8	9	10
1										
2										
3										
4										
5										
6										
7										
8										
9										
10										

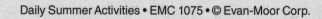

142

Letter Formation Chart

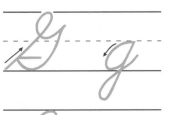  

 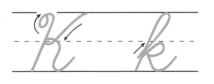

  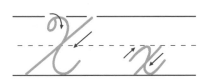